Published by Life Bliss Foundation, Bangalore, India

First Edition: December 2006
Second Edition: July 2007

ISBN 13: 978-1-934364-14-7 ISBN 10: 1-934364-14-2

All proceeds from the sales of this book go towards supporting Life Bliss Foundation's charitable activities.

Printed in India by Adwit (India) Pvt. Limited, Bangalore.

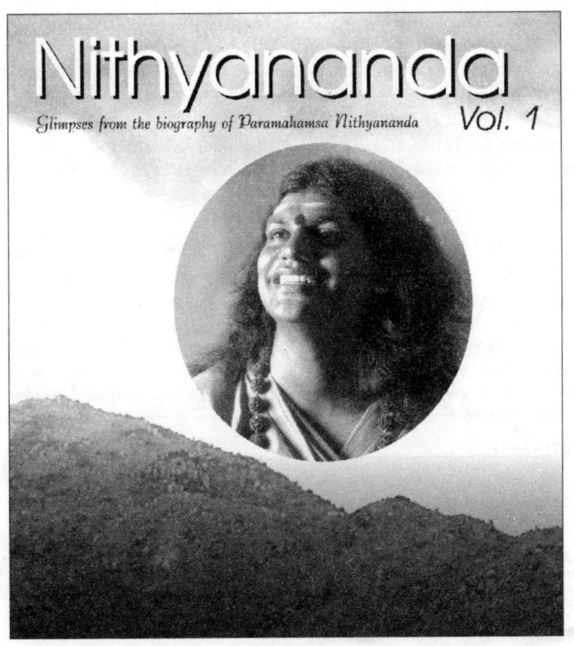
Nithyananda
Vol. 1
Glimpses from the biography of Paramahamsa Nithyananda

In Gratitude

This account of Nithyananda's life is a labor of love and gratitude. The words flowed from the Master. The writing work that went in was only to put these words down on paper, or as in this case, in Word documents in laptops.

It is said that the great Hindu epic Mahabharata was narrated by the sage Vyasa, and that it was written down by Lord Ganesa without a pause. In the case of Nithyananda's biography, unlike the Mahabharata, there was no need really for a Ganesa to transcribe the Master's own Vyasa-like renderings. In this day and age, recording and transcribing gadgets with appropriate voice recognition software could have easily done the job. It was the Master's compassion and love that allowed us to be instruments and partners in this creative process. We feel deep gratitude for the boundless compassion of our dear Master. What we absorbed during this process was immeasurable and could not have been imbibed in any other way. The process was truly one of deep meditation.

This is a biographical account of a unique Master. His persona transcends all classifications of nationalities, cultures, religions, political affiliations or social status. Most importantly, He is a Master who transcends any attempt to frame Him, whether as a Master, or as a friend, or as a mother, or as a child, or as a beloved. He is mercurial, forever changing and keeps us flexible too. He lives with us in form and in his formless energy, sharing His love, joy, energy and laughter. His appeal is universal and his message timeless.

Throughout this introduction, the Master's name will appear as nithyananda – in lower case - when talking about him in his pre-enlightenment period. This is deliberate, not an error of proof reading! Referring to Him with a capital H is also not a typo! Nor is it a ploy to confuse the reader. A Master, the Master, according to Hindu scriptures is the same energy as the Divine; in fact He is greater than Divine.

Hindu scriptures say that whatever even the Creator has determined for us, can be erased and rewritten by the little toe of the Master. To Him, that Divine energy we bow!

The entire purpose of Nithyananda's life is to lead people spiritually upwards and transform them into blissful beings, un-clutched from the play of the mind and centered in their core within. This volume, which offers glimpses of His biography, has many soul-stirring events, which have ignited and are continuing to ignite transformation and fulfillment in many. It is presented with the hope to inspire one to pursue his teachings and techniques, which are really formulae to put one into the state of Nithyananda - which literally means Eternal Bliss!

As the Master says:

A scientist is one who gives a formula to create the same experience that he had in the outer world for others to experience.

A Master is one who gives a formula to create the same experience that he had in the inner world for others to experience.

This volume the first in a series, is written to present to the readers glimpses of the life of a revolutionary Master who continues to touch and transform millions of lives, who presents life solutions through formulae from His own experience of the Ultimate Truth.

In this first volume of Nithyananda's biography, His birth and childhood are covered. This book ends at the point when He leaves home. In later volumes that will be written in the months to come, details of His parivrajaka (days of wandering), His enlightenment, and a few years after His enlightenment when the mission was born, will be covered.

As He says, 'Reading or listening to a Master's life story is an invaluable meditation, which can simply put you into the deep experience behind the words.'

If you can keep an open and curious mind, as that of a child, neither accepting nor rejecting, but just letting the words flow into your Being, if you can open yourself to the exploration and experience as a curious child would, you will discover that the following pages are exciting discoveries of your own Self.

We intend that this book, an account of the life of an enlightened Master, serves as a source of inspiration for the readers to delve deep into the inner self and create awareness about their own purpose in life.

- NAA

Contents

Chapter - 1

Master :
The Master Surgeon

Who are we?

Buddha had said that it is a great gift to be born as a human being; that it is even a greater gift to seek the Spiritual Truth of one's own inner nature in this human birth. But the greatest gift, Buddha said, is the opportunity to come in contact with an enlightened Master in one's lifetime and to stay with him.

The Master is available. It is the disciple who hesitates. Caught between the webs of what we wish the world around us to be and the greed to fulfill the unending desires that we have been indulging in since childhood, we forget our inner nature. We forget who we are. We hesitate when the Master calls. We become afraid.

A small story:

There once was a lioness, which was heavily pregnant, out on a hunt. As she chased a herd of sheep she slipped and was injured. As she died she gave birth to a cub. The lioness had died far from her pride, and the cub was all alone and helpless. As it struggled to get up and walk around, some of the sheep that passed by took pity on it and adopted it. The lion cub grew up with the sheep, played with them, drank goat's milk, fed on grass and other vegetable matter, and even learnt to bleat. He was now no longer a lion but just another sheep in the herd. He was quite happy eating grass and bleating along with the other sheep.

One day a lion attacked the sheep herd. This lion was shocked to find a lion cub in the herd. He was so shocked that he gave up thoughts of killing any of the sheep. He was curious to know more about the lion cub that had become part of a sheep herd.

The lion came by the next day and waited till the lion cub was at a distance from the herd. He quickly pounced on the cub and took him away carrying him by his throat. The cub nearly died of fear. He could not even bleat, so great was his fear. The lion put him down after a while and told him that he was not a sheep, but was really a lion. The cub had no understanding of what he was being told. To him, reality was that he was a sheep and a lion was a mortal enemy. The cub kept bleating: let me go, let me go. The lion was wise and patient. He took him back to the herd and left him there, the cub still shaking in fright.

The lion came back every day and picked up the cub. Each day he would tell the cub who he really was; that he was a lion and not a sheep. The cub was not convinced; he did not even know what the lion was talking about. Yet by now the cub realized that the lion meant him no harm and allowed himself to be carried by him. Now and then he would get scared and plead with the lion to let him go. He would even run away. Nevertheless, the lion would pick him up and talk to him again about his true nature.

After many such outings, the lion took the cub to a stream one day and made him look at his own reflection in the water. The cub looked in the water, saw his reflection. What he saw was a lion staring back at him. Bewildered and terrified, the cub bleated in great fear and ran as fast as his legs would carry him. The lion brought him back gently to the water again and explained to him who he really was; that he was no sheep but a lion. The cub looked into the water again and again. He looked around and saw that there was no one else around him; the reflection was his own. Next, the lion gave him a piece of meat to eat. The cub ate it and found an instant liking to it.

Suddenly the cub realized who he was and let out a roar. He became a lion at that moment.

Many of us are like the lion cub. We have forgotten who we are. Societal conditioning has robbed us of the truth of our Being, the truth of our own inner nature. We see ourselves as sheep instead of the lions that we are.

Role of the Master

When a Master comes by and tells us who we are, rather than being deeply grateful for being given the truth, we bleat in mortal fear and run as fast as we can. *He tells us that we are not ordinary human beings looking for spiritual experience but spiritual beings looking for human experience.* However, we are not ready to believe him. The Master becomes an enemy, not a savior. He indeed becomes the *simha swapna*, the lion-dream or the nightmare to us. We even think that he is trying to convert us to some exclusive religion! We play hide and seek with him.

A few of us start realizing a little of what we are and what we can be after a few encounters with him. We then allow the Master to play with us and start feeling a certain level of comfort. He then behaves like one among us to make us feel more comfortable. Then, one day, when our trust has grown to a steady state, the Master grabs us and shows us who we really are, that he and we are the same.

The Master's play - his *lila*, is one of infinite compassion. It is the only unconditional love that there is upon this planet. The only purpose of this love is to show us who we really are; to tear the mask of the sheep that we have so far worn and to reveal the lion within us; to make us roar instead of bleat; to de-hypnotize us from the illusions we have lived with so far. The Master leads us into reality, into bliss, into our true nature.

To most of us, this process is a surgery that is painful to our psyche. We would much rather be comfortable with the sheep's form that we are used to than undergo the surgery and be exposed to what we think are the dangers of realizing the lion's form that is truly ours. The Master's work is to remove the cancerous tumor of our Being, which is called Ego. It is this ego, the identity that we have built for ourselves based on past experiences that prevents us from realizing that we are lions. But our mind continuously resists his work, for the surgery on our ego is too much to take. It is like operating to remove our very life-sustaining element. 'How can I lose my identity', our mind resists!

We say, 'Let us be happy with what we are, how we are. What if the world is an illusion; it is an addictive illusion; we are busy with the silly things we do every day; we cry, we laugh; we are joyful; we are depressed; sheep have their good points; they are cute and lovable; who wants to be a lion anyway; all our friends and family will run away. Who needs to be in bliss? What is bliss anyway?'

To those of us who think like this, the Master then becomes the enemy. We would rather be with the cancer that we know, than with the new Being that we do not know anything about.

Realizing the truth of who we are requires courage. Moving away from societal and religious beliefs and conditioning, takes great courage. To get ourselves de-hypnotized from the bondages that we are so happily ensconced in requires wisdom and determination. To become a lion from being a sheep is a physical transformation and a mental alchemy that requires fixity of purpose that not all of us possess or even want to possess.

It requires courage to trust the Master. This trust when happens, becomes over time, total acceptance and surrender. Only at this point are we ready to learn the truth about ourselves. Only at this point has real conviction about the truth happened in us.

We are all saints within

What we do in real life and what our status is in real life have no relevance to the fundamental truth of our own inner nature. The inner nature of a saint and sinner are the same. Society applies these labels to us at its convenience and comfort. Someone labeled as a sinner has as much potential to realize the truth himself as someone who considers himself holy.

Valmiki was a renowned saint of ancient India. He was the author of one of the greatest Hindu epics, the Ramayana, which is read and enjoyed not only in India but also in many parts of South and South East Asia.

Valmiki was a thief who became a saint. Narada, a great devotee of Lord Vishnu - the Preserver in the Hindu Trinity of Gods - was a wandering minstrel saint. Narada forever traveled the skies chanting the name of 'Narayana' (one of Vishnu's 1008 names). Once he happened to cross Valmiki's path, when he was still a dreaded thief. Narada was promptly stopped by Valmiki who demanded money from him. Narada had no money with him. This made Valmiki furious. He threatened Narada that he would kill him if he did not come up with something valuable at once.

Narada had nothing on him except the simple clothes he wore and the single stringed instrument that he strummed on, as he sang the praises of Lord Vishnu. Narada told him that the only thing valuable he had with him was the mantra 'Narayana' that he constantly uttered. Narada offered to teach him this mantra which would lead him to salvation. Narada said, 'Chant this mantra and when you die, you will not die alone; the Lord will be with you.'

Valmiki was not impressed. He said, 'In any case I shall not die alone. I have my entire family who will readily join me; I live for them. I steal for them. I have no need for your mantra. Unless you come up with something valuable I shall kill you.'

Narada pleaded with him and finally said, 'Please go and ask your family members which one of them will walk with you to the gates of death. If they say as you believe that they will accompany you to the gates of death, come back and kill me.'

Valmiki proudly strutted off, believing Narada's word that he would not run away. Valmiki went home and asked his son, whom he dearly loved and who loved him in return, 'Son, when death beckons, will you join me?'

The son was shocked. He said, 'No, of course not! You are old and it is time for you to go. I have a life. Don't you think that you should let me be?'

Valmiki was shattered. Yet, without showing any emotion, he approached his wife who he was sure would be with him always, and asked her whether she would accompany him at the time of death. His wife hesitated and told him tenderly, 'Dear, we need one of us to stay to look after our children. If you go, and I go with you, who will take care of them?'

Valmiki then approached his old parents and asked them. They too refused to go with him; they wanted to live for some more years.

Valmiki was in tears. He went back to Narada and narrated to him what happened and cried piteously. Narada comforted him and said, 'No one will come with you, nothing will come with you; none of your relatives, none of your possessions. You will go alone when death calls you. The only thing that can go with you is the name of the Lord.' Saying this, he initiated him into the mantra of 'Narayana'.

As soon as Valmiki uttered the word 'Narayana', he realized his true Self, and sank into a deep meditative state, a samadhi, and stayed on in that samadhi state for hundreds of years. An anthill grew on top of him, and no one knew there was someone under the anthill. When he finally emerged from his samadhi from inside the anthill, Valmiki was an enlightened sage. In Sanskrit, Valmiki means 'anthill', and was called by that name ever since.

Inside of each sinner there is a saint waiting to emerge. The work of a Master is bringing out the saint.

Discontentment leads to the Master

It is easy to have a casual relationship with the Master, dropping in whenever it suits you. It is comfortable to come with the pretense that you would spend more time plumbing the depths of your inner Self with the help of the Master at some point in time in the future. You tell yourself that it will all happen when the time is right, without realizing that the right time is now.

People look for many things from a Master. 90% of the people are in search of material benefits from him, in the same way as they are in a temple praying before the idol. In the temple, we all become beggars. In fact, we reduce the deities we pray to beggar's status by bargaining with them and negotiating payments. We promise the deity a percentage of benefits received in return. We say, 'I need a million dollars and I shall give you 20% in return if you give me a million dollars. If you like, take that 20% up front, and give me only the balance.' The material benefits may vary from direct financial gains to improvement in health to providing a child to the childless to seeking salvation. We beg the Gods in the temple. We carry with us the same beggar's attitude to the Master also.

In both the cases, when we get what we begged for, we realize too late that what we begged for and were given, are things that we could have done without, which are really not what we want at a deep level, at the level of the Being. But we don't understand why we feel this way; we don't understand why there is no deep satisfaction and we continue begging for other material things. The cycle goes on.

Human beings are not created for material pleasures alone. In all of us is an inbuilt homing device that seeks the original state we all come from. That state is the state of divinity, the state of the Universal energy, Universal intelligence that maintains order amongst all the chaos that seemingly surrounds us. That is why however much we may indulge in sensual pleasures, there is no fulfillment; it is always more and more; and yet, the more we indulge the more we need; the less we are content. Indulging in sensual pleasures alone is an addiction; as deeply dissatisfying as any addiction. This deep discontent within all of us, discontent with mere sensual and material pleasures, is the seed of spirituality that seeks a higher experience, a more fulfilling experience, a spiritual experience.

Few people approach the Master with a learning perspective, either intellectual or spiritual. In the West, the search for a Master is really a cure for the 'depression of success' born out of a surfeit of material success that becomes an imbalance with one's spiritual needs that lie deep inside. People in the West try to cope with this by constant change; they change cars every year, homes every second year and spouses every third year! Then, they are surprised that they still do not find satisfaction.

In India, people come to a Master out of 'depression of failure'; they seek mostly in material terms. They are still unfulfilled not having got what they wanted; so they strive. Depression of failure is easier to resolve than depression of success.

Many of us have an active dissatisfaction with what we find around us, in terms of lack of ethics and morality. This dissatisfaction, this gap between the need for a higher value system and what we find ourselves in, prompts some of us into positive action of one kind or another.

The reference to the value system here is not to religious value systems of ethics and morality, which are created by society. It refers to the inner consciousness of the individual, which is the only solution to all the problems faced in the material world. A clear consciousness in each individual can create a blissful and peaceful planet Earth.

In today's corporate world, like balloons pressured beyond what they can bear, we can see corporate leaders burst with pressure, damaging themselves and others around them. Yet, there are a few who we meet who maintain their balance despite all the pressures. These few are like the proverbial reeds in Tao that bend with the water and get back to position once the pressure of water recedes.

It helps when one has a balanced perspective of one's own capabilities against what one has been able to achieve; to take from life what it offers rather than keep looking for what we think it should offer.

Whatever success we manage to achieve in life has little to do with our own abilities. There were and are many others who are more intelligent than we are; more decisive, more caring and more dynamic, who probably did not reach the same levels of material success as we measure these factors of success and status with. On the contrary, we see around us intellectual, emotional and spiritual people who are far more successful materially and professionally.

There is a factor that goes beyond one's inherited powers, education, innate capabilities, DNA and whatever else that one can measure within oneself that contributes to what one achieves in life, both materially and spiritually. Is that *karma*, fate or destiny or is it a spiritual quotient that can measure our evolution in spiritual terms? Why am I what I am? Where am I headed? What is my purpose in life? Who am I?

This desire to move beyond and also to understand who we are, still drives many of us. It is this creative tension that brings us to a Master. It is this creative tension that draws us again and again to the Master against the resistance of our mind.

Nithyananda is a spiritual Master who is truly irreverent of religious hypocrisy; one who addresses practical issues of how to live one's life day to day, hour to hour, minute to minute and second to second; one who doesn't convince through scriptural or religious sanctioned lore, but through just His presence and His own experience of the Ultimate Truth; one who brings to bear His experiential wisdom that transcended His youthful years; far more importantly who through His sheer grace and energy brings us warmth and brightness that we have never before experienced.

In front of Him, our questions evaporate. To sit in front of Him in silence is meditation.
He says that meeting Him is never an accident.
Meeting the Master is the purpose of life while nothing else in life itself is of any direct purpose.

Master – the Master Surgeon

Most of us think that we have a clear purpose that we believe in and lead our lives in line with and in anticipation of achieving that purpose, till time and time again we realize that the purpose seems impermanent. It keeps changing. When we achieve that purpose to which we had been willing to dedicate our entire life, we are still unfulfilled. We are discontent. The true nature of a human being is that it can never be satisfied with material achievements. The Self seeks more; it seeks the Master.

Then we meet the Master. Like many of us met Nithyananda. Many of us are whom He calls professional seekers, who till meeting Him had not found answers to the hundreds of questions that continually addressed the value of our beliefs, knowledge and experience. The questions we had simply disappeared when we met Him. There were doubts and there continue to be doubts, but no questions anymore. They seem to get answered before they arise.

Many of us in professional careers achieved most of what we set out to do materially and then wondered why we wanted all that in the first place. Acquisition brought only a momentary pleasure. As that pleasure waned, we needed to begin the next chase to keep ourselves occupied in the pursuit of what we imagined to be our next port of call of happiness. 'What next?' was almost always the question, even before we had had time to absorb and reflect upon what we had achieved and acquired.

Nithyananda lights a lamp within us that dispels the darkness of ignorance layer upon layer that we have accumulated through our lives.

The Upanishad says: *Tamaso ma jyotirgamaya.* It means, 'lead us from darkness to light.' It is with this helpless plea that we come to the Master.

It is his grace that holds our hands as we traverse that path of light.

The Master is a master surgeon. He cuts through the cancers of our ego and falsehood and exposes us mercilessly to the reality of our true nature. The closer we come to him the hotter it gets.

Nithyananda says,

'When you come to me as a stranger, as a window shopper, I am happy to offer you brain candy, and you can taste the sweetness and go away. When you seek and come near, you become my responsibility. It is my promise to you to show you your true Self. My compassion to my near and dear is tough on them at times!'

The presence of a living Master is the ultimate gift that there is. God to most of us is a concept; for some to ridicule; for many to worship. There is no common understanding of what one needs to do to approach God. Religions, rather religious leaders, who are supposed to guide us to God, are the biggest sinners in this regard. They divide and rule. They fight and destroy. To one, an idol is essential to reach God; to another, idols are improper; to each, his scripture and his brand of God is the only path to salvation.

Although each authentic religion was created with the same idea of realizing God within, over time, this underlying purpose of religion has been forgotten and focus has shifted to the regulatory paths that were devised in each religion to control through fear and greed. People are termed sinners so that they can be subjugated. Fanaticism and terrorism through religion have replaced salvation through it!

The Ultimate Truth is the same in all religions. Once this truth is realized, the shackles of religion drop off.

With a real Master, inner growth happens in us without any religious compulsions. Neither is there any compulsive binding between the Master and disciple from the Master's side.

Nithyananda says,

'Go to as many Masters as you wish to, but learn something worthwhile from each of them. Go to as many gardens as you want to and collect the most beautiful flowers from them and make a garland for yourself!

People go to many Masters but the problem is they don't learn anything from any of them. They are simply window shoppers who come, look in and go away. Or, they come and get clutched to the Master's personality instead of his teachings and start creating trouble in society. Or they get frightened by the Master's tough love and seek another who would be easier on them.

When Jesus Christ and Lord Krishna meet each other, they will hug each other, as they are both enlightened Masters. However, the sheep that follow Jesus and the cows that follow Krishna will always end up fighting as to whose Master was greater!'

Again, this is fanaticism in the name of Masters instead of in the name of religion; no great difference.

This book is an inspirational account of Nithyananda's life to show the path that he traversed, to kindle in us the desire to seek the true nature of our own inner Self. This book has only one purpose, which is to show us that we are indeed lions, not sheep.

As Nithyananda says time and again:

I am not here to prove *I* am God; I am here to prove *you* are God.

Truth and Fact:

Sukha Brahma, the great sage and the young son of Vyasa - author of the Hindu epic Mahabharata - was teaching many great sages far older than him. He narrated to them the Bhagavatam - story of the ten incarnations of Lord Vishnu and specifically that of His incarnation as Krishna.

At the end of it, moved to tears, one of the assembled rishis fell at Sukha Brahma's feet and said passionately, 'Please do not put any of this in writing. Once set in writing, in words, the deep truth, the intense beauty, which can never be expressed in words, will be lost. No one will then know really what happened here. No one will ever be able to experience through reading the words, the energy play that happened here during the narration, the spirit behind the words, the experience of our souls in listening to you. The facts will completely belittle the truth and energy in the whole thing.'

Sukha said, 'I agree with you; but we need to write all this down, so that future generations may become inspired by just reading it. The words will be a great source of inspiration and a driving force to every soul that reads it. It will drive them to experience the truth behind the words; that is enough.'

The reason why we have written an account of our Master's life is the same. It is true that the truth, the experiential truth, cannot be captured in words. Yet, this experiential truth, when expressed however inadequately, can inspire millions.

Facts are chronological details as found in history. The West has always been interested in facts; in chronology; in history; in what can be verified through some means. Western science needs to prove things with the intellect; it has to prove things with logic in order to present it to the world. The East is more focused on truth.

Truth however is metaphorical, not factual; it transcends time and space; it cannot be proved by straight logic. If logic can prove the truth, then logic has to be greater than the truth, which can never be! This biography offers both the truth and the facts to the best extent possible.

Ramayana is the well-known Hindu epic that Valmiki wrote of the great King Rama, an incarnation of Lord Vishnu. In this story, Rama's wife Sita is kidnapped by a demon king Ravana. Rama while on his pursuit of Ravana seeks the help of the monkeys who lived in the forest kingdom of Kishkinda. This kingdom was ruled by the monkey brothers Vali and Sugriva, assisted by the redoubtable Hanuman, who is worshipped as the monkey God all over India.

When Valmiki described Kishkinda in Ramayana, he provided a certain number for the monkey population. If literally taken, the number Valmiki provided might not at all match the size of Kishkinda as he had described it. Kishkinda could not have held that many millions of monkeys. When Valmiki referred to such a number, it was in a *puranic* sense of the truth, a metaphorical representation of the truth. Valmiki was conveying the power of the monkeys through the number, not the exact number of monkeys.

The number connotes the strength he was talking about.

Valmiki's visualization was truth-oriented. Valmiki referred to the energy of the monkeys through the number, not the number itself. Valmiki's focus was on the truth of the energy rather than the factual representation.

Science would like everything verified and quantified. This does not mean that what science has not verified and quantified is not true. The law of gravity operated ever since creation; it was in existence since Existence; otherwise the Sun and the planets would not move as they have done always. Yet, Newton 'discovered' gravity only a few centuries ago, and society and religion, till then unaware of this 'discovery' accepted it as a scientific fact. The earth has always been round; that has been the truth; yet this truth was bitterly contested and finally agreed upon only in the last millennium.

Science is limited in perception. It is like trying to explore a dense and dark forest with a small lamp. The lamp shows a few feet ahead and science comes up with one theory based on what it sees for those few feet. Next, they move ahead with the light and see a few more feet. What they see now is different from what they saw earlier. So they come up with a new theory and discard the one that they proposed earlier. This is how science operates. But imagine, if the whole forest was visible in one flash of lightning! This is how enlightened Masters see the whole thing, the whole truth. This is the difference between science and mysticism.

People over centuries have suffered many misgivings because the truth they saw within their beings did not match with the truth as accepted by society and organized religion.

When an enlightened Master is asked how old he is, his chronological, factually correct answer would be far different from the truth of his timeless existence.

In this book, an attempt has been made to bring both chronological and historical facts together with the existential truth. Facts are limited by the 120-degree vision that we are normally capable of. Truth is a spiritual 360-degree vision that only enlightened Masters have. This book presents an enlightened Master's 360-degree vision, which we should strive to perceive with as little distortion as possible. This book is factually factful, and truthfully truthful. It is a meeting of the Eastern system of mysticism and the western system of logic.

Facts and truth do not always go together; facts are one-dimensional, relating only to time, whereas truth is space and time; it is multidimensional.

In *Nithyananda* - Eternal Bliss, truth and facts merge.

Chapter - 2

Arunachala: The Spiritual Incubator

In the song 'Akshara manamaalai', the great enlightened Master, Bhagwan Ramana Maharishi sings thus towards Arunachala, the Divine Hillock which is a manifestation of the Siva Energy:

Oh Arunachala! Tell me, who is more intelligent between the two of us? I gave myself to you, a being without any earthly gain or heavenly value, and got you, the Divine in return!

As snow in water, dissolve me in your form, which is pure love.

Legend of Arunachala: Siva resolves dispute between Vishnu and Brahma

Tiruvannamalai is a small town in South India in the state of Tamil Nadu.

'Tiru Anna Malai' as it should be termed in chaste Tamil, the name of this place means 'Revered Inaccessible Mountain'. This name was given to this town not because it was the location of a tall and mighty mountain, being more a medium sized hillock, but because of the spiritual connotation that the place had for believers and spiritual seekers. The entire township has evolved around the mountain and a '*girivalam*' or walking around the mountain on foot, is considered to be holy and spiritually value enhancing.
In Sanskrit, this mountain is termed 'Arunachala', literally meaning the 'Unmoving Morning Star', simplified as the 'Red Mountain', possibly in reference to its reddish hue. *Aruna*, the morning star, is the charioteer of the Sun God Surya. *Aruna* drives a magnificent chariot yoked to seven white horses that Surya rides in.

Sages from time immemorial are reputed to have lived in the caves and slopes of the Arunachala hill, sanctified by it and sanctifying it in turn. Adi Sankara, the great Hindu reformer saint, had described Arunachala as Mount Meru, the inaccessible heart center of Lord Siva. Arunachala reveals itself as no ordinary mountain. It beholds timeless majesty and a shroud of mystery that centuries of legend have only deepened. Arunachala has a presence that is more spiritual than physical. The great enlightened Master Bhagwan Sri Ramana Maharishi calls Arunachala 'the spiritual center of the world.'

It is not for nothing that Arunachala is known as the 'hill that beckons'. Even the ordinary traveler, once having set his eyes upon Arunachala, is drawn inexplicably to dwell upon its sacred presence again and again. This strange experience, known as 'the call of Arunachala', is commonly felt by seekers even today.

The legend of Arunachala, and the story behind the temple of Arunachaleshwara which is the central point of the town of Tiruvannamalai, reads thus:

In ancient Hindu mythology, there is a story of an argument between Lord Brahma, the Creator and Lord Vishnu the Sustainer, as to who was greater. Brahma and Vishnu are two out of the three Gods who comprise the Trinity of the Hindu pantheon of divinity. They were unable to resolve the dispute amongst themselves. There was no one to resolve the fight except Siva, the Rejuvenator, and the third member of this Divine Trinity.

Siva appeared before them in his Vishwa Rupa - the Divine form - in such a Herculean size, as a shaft of light, that the two ends of the shaft that were his head and feet could not be seen.
He looked at them and said: whoever can find either of my ends is the greater of the two of you. So Brahma went up towards the head in the form of a flying swan and Vishnu went downwards as a boar, digging below the ground to find Siva's feet. They searched for ages, many yugas – periods of Time. Vishnu realized at some point that he could not find what he sought and decided to surrender his ego at that point. He told Siva to forgive his arrogance in trying to look for his feet. Siva blessed him for his honesty.

*Brahma, however, could not accept his failure. On his way up, he saw a flower (*screwpine or *taazham poo in Tamil) falling down and asked the flower where it was coming from. The flower said it had fallen from Siva's ears. Brahma asked, 'How long have you been traveling?' The flower replied, 'I have been falling for four ages of Brahma!' Brahma was shocked and realized he had no hopes of finding Siva's head, but he still did not want to accept his failure.*

Brahma decided that he would tell Siva a lie about finding this flower on his ear. He then asked the flower to bear witness that he had brought it down from Siva's head. The flower hesitated, but Brahma persuaded it to tell this lie saying that in any case Siva would not know. The flower, having little choice, and afraid to refuse Brahma – the Lord of all Creation, agreed. Both went down to Siva and Brahma told Siva that he had seen Siva's head and brought this flower as his witness.

Siva instantly knew what had happened and was angry at the lie told to him. He punished Brahma saying, 'for the lie that you have uttered, you will be never be worshipped by the people.' He punished the screwpine flower saying, 'You will never ever be used as an offering to me in my puja.' To this day, there are no major temples dedicated to Brahma, the Creator; and the screwpine flower is never offered to Siva in worship. Brahma realized his mistake and sought Siva's forgiveness. Both Vishnu and Brahma requested Siva to keep his form as that shaft of light to bless the Universe.

At their request, Siva in that Divine Light form became Arunachala, the glowing mountain and assumed the form of the 'jyotirlingam' called Arunachaleshwara, at the temple in Tiruvannamalai.

Temple of Arunachaleshwara: Largest Siva Temple

Siva is traditionally worshipped by Hindus in the form of the *lingam*, which literally means gender or sex, and by extension refers to the male sexual organ, specifically by religious connotation to *Siva*. In truth, the *lingam* refers to the act of creation as well as that of rejuvenation, which is the cycle of birth, death and rebirth. The *lingam* therefore is an integration of the male and female, *Siva* and *Sakti*, nature and energy.

In construction, the *lingam* idol is a combination of the male and female sexual organs, with esoteric integration with the other two members of the Hindu mythological Trinity, that are Brahma - the Creator, and Vishnu - the Sustainer. In a few places, Siva, in the form of the *lingam*, is visualized as the elemental energy such as light or fire.

The temple of Arunachaleshwara in Tiruvannamalai, is the biggest temple to Siva in India. It is one of the five sacred *lingam* sites of Siva in South India. Here Siva is worshipped in His elemental form of fire, as one of the *pancha bhutas* - the five elements of nature. These five elemental energies are: earth, water, fire, air and ether.

The other Siva temple sites where He is worshipped in His elemental form are: Chidambaram where Siva is worshipped as ether or space, Kalahasti where He is worshipped as air, Kanchipuram where He is worshipped as earth, and Tiruvanaikkaval where He is worshipped as water. It is also believed that Siva appeared to His consort Parvati here in Arunachala as a column of fire on a *Karthikai Purnima* day

(*Karthikai* is the Tamil month of November-December and *Purnima* is the full moon day), when she prayed to unite with Him.

The temple of Arunachala has been sung about in Tamil in the 7th century by the Tamil Saint Thirugnana Sambandar, and is believed to have existed since long before. It is built in a combination of three distinct architectural styles:

The inner sanctum and first courtyard are of the style of the Chola kings of the 9th century. The later day Chola kings of the 11th century added an additional *prahara* (courtyard) and *gopuram* (entrance tower) with grand carvings. The third *prahara* and the massive fourteen-storey tower are from the Vijayanagaram style of the 16th century, begun by king Krishna Devaraya. The later day extensions (there are seven courtyards in all) have been carried out in total harmony with the original Chola structure that makes this temple one of the finest examples of Dravidian architecture. This temple of Arunachala has nine towers on its four walls, the eastern and largest *gopuram* being 72 meters tall with thirteen levels in it.

In the traditional style of town planning in the Southern parts of India, the temple is the centerpiece, much as a Church is in many older towns or Town halls in newer ones in the West. Almost always, temples were square or rectangular structures in plan, with many such squares and rectangles built one within the other depending on the size. Many of the great temples in South India are many acres in size, the Tiruvannamalai temple being nearly 20 acres in size.

At the centre of the temple structure is the altar to the ruling Divinity, God or Goddess, the sanctum sanctorum, called *garba graham*, or womb space. All temples have high walls, tall towers on each of the four sides and spacious roads that border the temple on all four sides. As the town grew, it developed around these four main roads, once again in a parallel path, square within a square, much as New York was planned in a grid-like fashion!

Some of us had the opportunity to visit Tiruvannamalai along with Nithyananda late in December 2005, on his star birthday based on the Hindu Vedic calendar. We walked around the temple early in the morning, as the town was still waking up. As the Master had asked us to, and in accordance with the Hindu custom of not wearing footwear inside any holy location such as a temple, we went without footwear, and basked in the sanctity of this holy space in the presence of the Master. Later that day, we had the once in a lifetime opportunity to be with the Master in the temple that he loved and grew up in.

Living Masters of Arunachala: Bhagwan Sri Ramana Maharishi

In recent times, Tiruvannamalai has been best known for Bhagwan Ramana Maharishi, one of the greatest saints and enlightened Masters of modern day India. Ramana moved into Tiruvannamalai when he was sixteen and lived in the ambience of the Arunachala hill for the rest of his mortal life. Known as the Silent Sage, Ramana communicated his message of enlightenment through the process of Self-enquiry. Though he never traveled out of Arunachala and spoke little, the sheer energy that he radiated along with his personal grace and charisma, attracted thousands to Tiruvannamalai. Many spiritual centers propagating Ramana's ideas have been set up in different parts of the world. A number of Western writers, including Somerset Maugham, visited Ramana and wrote about him. Ramana called Arunachala, 'the spiritual center of the world'.

Ramana's process of Self-enquiry leads one to the source of one's thoughts. Ramana says to keep asking: Who Am I? This query and enquiry peels through layers of the mind and body and leads ultimately to the Realization that what one truly is, is not the body, not the mind, not anything material, but the inner spirit and the inner divinity. This process when carried out experientially, and not as an intellectual exercise, leads to Self Realization. More than the process, it was the grace, the presence of Ramana, the Master, an incarnation, which enlightened the disciples who were gathered around him.

Ramana's philosophy of Self-enquiry has inspired many present day thinkers including Eckhardt Tolle, whose brilliant and seminal book 'Power of Now' takes part of its roots from Ramana.

Arunachala is a spiritual incubator. When a Master enters this world in a human body, his state is too pure to withstand the rigors of daily life upon this planet. His purity has to be alloyed, as it were, with human attributes, so that the physical form can survive upon planet Earth.

Just like how a clinical incubator preserves a baby, a spiritual incubator is needed to provide these enlightened beings with the right ambience to shield them, so to speak, from any disruption to their highly evolved state. This incubator ensures that the spirit is sustained as close to the purest, attribute less levels as is possible in human reality, so that the enlightened being can live within its human form, yet retaining most of its pure quality. Arunachala serves as a spiritual incubator to enlightened beings, who descend upon planet Earth.

Ramakrishna says, 'Dozens of flies crowd around a cow all day, but they only drink its blood; it is only the calf that comes in, perhaps twice a day, goes straight to its mother's udder and drinks milk and returns.' Enlightened Masters are like the calf that comes to imbibe the milk of spirituality that Arunachala beholds.

Time and again, Tiruvannamalai has given birth to enlightened Masters who have touched and transformed millions of seekers in the world.

Why Enlightened Masters are buried and not cremated

Arunachala has been the spiritual incubator that has provided the nurturing for many enlightened Masters over thousands of years. It has the lineage of a great enlightened Master Arunagiri Yogishwara, embodiment of Lord Siva Himself. The massive temple of Tiruvannamalai is built on the *jiva samadhi* (burial place of the body and living spirit of an enlightened Master) of Arunagiri Yogishwara. Prayers are offered to Yogishwara first in this temple, even before the ruling deity that is Arunachaleshwara. Ramana refers to Yogishwara, the great Master, as a young sage sitting under a banyan tree teaching many older persons seated around him.

In the Hindu tradition, enlightened Masters are always buried, whereas the bodies of others are always burnt. There is a scientific background to this practice. Bodies are the receptacle of our desires, and our embedded memories, called *samskara. Samskara* is the collection of emotional experiences that build themselves into value systems and beliefs, which drive our lives, often unconsciously. Collection of these memories begin well before our birth and last even after our death.

Studies by Dr. Bruce Lipton, the eminent cellular biologist, have now shown at the cellular level, that the embryo in the mother's womb retains memories of what transpires in the outer world. Interaction between parents and the emotional state of the parents, especially the mother, are carried viscerally into the infant through its cellular structure.

Similarly, memories live on after we die, and these memories are embedded in the body. If the body is buried, these memories stay on at the place of burial and remain intangibly present.

It is possible that in cultures where the dead are buried, the practice started with purification rituals that ensured the removal of memories from the bodies being buried. In the absence of such practices, which may no longer be followed, there is a possibility that the memories stay on even as the body decomposes. The intangible presence of these memories is what one would perceive as ghosts and spirits.

The feelings of some people who are sensitive to these super natural sensations are very real; the experience is not hallucination. Whether we believe it or not, understand it or not, accept it or not, memories survive our death and linger on.

In the case of enlightened Masters, their memories are very powerful and value enhancing. What they leave behind in their bodies are enormous amounts of energy. Hindus believe that this energy of enlightened Masters can be preserved by burying their bodies under the right conditions in a living tomb, called the *jiva samadhi.*

Jiva samadhis of great Masters are spiritually and enormously powerful; they are pure energy; they are the equivalent of nuclear reactors.

Nithyananda says that in his personal experience he has seen five such *jiva samadhis* of Masters who lived in India until recently: Raghavendra Swami in Mantralaya, Saibaba at Shirdi, Bhagwan Ramana Maharishi at Tiruvannamalai, Ramakrishna *Paramahamsa* at Dakshineshwar, and Sadasiva Brahmendra at Nerur.

Siva's Presence in Arunachala: Promise to stay in 3 forms

Arunachala Purana - the legend of Arunachala - says that Lord Siva made a promise that He will always be available on this planet Earth in Arunachala in three forms: As the hill Arunachala; as the *jyotirlinga* Arunachaleshwara in the temple; and in the form of incarnated living Masters in this holy town of Tiruvannamalai; this truth has been reaffirmed by Ramana Maharishi.

The hill Arunachala lives on. Geologically this hill is considered older than the Himalayan range. The *Jyotirlingam* in the temple of Arunachaleshwara is worshipped by millions. Each full moon day, a million people gather at Tiruvannamalai to visit the temple and to walk around the hill. The living Masters of Arunachala come in as incarnations to fulfill their cosmic missions and depart when their mission is accomplished. This great temple town, by being the planet's spiritual incubator, ensures the continued presence of spirituality on planet Earth through the promise made by Siva.

Tiruvannamalai is a town that celebrates each day of the year as a temple festival day. In this town, every household takes pride in looking after ascetics and mendicants equally as they would sages and saints. Beggars are not looked down upon in this holy place. They are seen to provide an opportunity for people to be charitable. In this holy town, it is not easy to distinguish between a great Master who has given up all, including his followers, and a beggar, because both wear the same minimal attire! Such is the greatness of simplicity of the Masters dwelling here.

The great temple here provides its people with an introduction to the Hindu religion with its elaborately carved mythological stories and the legends that have grown around the town and the temple. The hill Arunachala radiates energy continuously and provides spiritual fulfillment. Living Masters who are always present here are like the bridge between the temple and the hill, thus fulfilling Siva's promise.

The theory of the inner science, the application of this inner science and the scientist who practices this inner space - all three happen here together at the same time and place! The hill represents the theory of the inner science – that is the *Sastra* - the sacred scriptures that cater to the intellect; the temple represents the application of it– that is the *Stotra* - the devotional verses that sing the praise of the Lord, catering to the faithful and the devotional followers who follow their emotions; and the living Masters are the scientists – that is the *Sutra* - the mystical techniques presented in epigrammatic form, that directly work at the level of the Being; they are the scientists who lead us to an understanding of the wisdom behind the theory, the timeless knowledge of which the Arunachala hill is a repository; and the path that they lead us through is the path of devotion to Arunachaleshwara, to the Divine that is Existence itself.

Siva continues to radiate His energy in Tiruvannamalai in all these three forms, blessing the world in line with His promise.

Who are Incarnations? Why do they take birth?

The vast majority of Hindus have a simple belief and faith in their Gods and Goddesses. They believe with their hearts and with deep emotion that these forms are real and are living forces. They also believe that Gods whom they visualize in various forms arrive on planet Earth as incarnations, or *avatar* as it is called, in human form from time to time. One could envision these incarnations as somewhat similar to what prophets are in Western religions. Real life stories, legends and epics are presented on these incarnations.

In the case of Lord Vishnu, the Conserver of the Universe in the Hindu Trinity, ten forms of *avatar* are chronicled in the epic *Bhagavatam*, told partly by the great sage Vyasa as a biographical account of the incarnations of Vishnu.

The mythology of the ten incarnations of Vishnu, in a sense, is the story of evolution of life forms. The story is one of the creation of the Universe and the ending of the Universe in a metaphoric sense. The sequence of the incarnations is the sequence of life forms upon planet Earth. The first incarnation is the fish incarnation - the *Matsya avatar*, depicting the origin of life from aquatic creatures. This is followed by the *Kurma avatar* - the tortoise incarnation, representing the next stage as an amphibian. The third is the *Varaha avatar* - the boar incarnation, representing a mammal. The fourth is the *Narasimha avatar* - half human and half lion form, half-way point to human form. The fifth incarnation is that of the dwarf - the *Vamana avatar*. The remaining five forms of incarnations are human representations, four of whom have come and gone: Rama, Krishna, Balarama and Buddha. The last that is Kalki, the warrior destroyer *avatar*, is yet to arrive upon planet Earth.

Of the human versions of the *Dasavatar* - the ten incarnations of Lord Vishnu - Krishna is considered to be the perfect incarnation or the *Purna avatar*. He is most widely and popularly known as the persona behind the Bhagavad Gita.

Hindus consider the Bhagavad Gita as the fifth *Veda*, the scriptural work that is on par with the four *Vedas* - books of knowledge that were revealed to enlightened sages. Bhagavad Gita is the dialogue between Lord Krishna, the eighth incarnation of Vishnu as the super conscious Divine Energy, and Arjuna, the Pandava Prince, who Lord Krishna takes to be his friend and disciple. In this dialogue, he delivers to Arjuna the Bhagavad Gita, as answers to his questions on worldly dilemma.

Arjuna's dilemma was in the middle of the battlefield, where he was about to be engaged in a destructive fight against his own cousins and teachers. He was not sure what the right thing to do was, whether to battle against those whom he had loved and respected or to walk away in surrender and apparent failure. Krishna explains to Arjuna what he should do and why he should do it. Krishna's timeless response to Arjuna is the substance of the Gita, as this book is popularly known. Krishna's message to Arjuna resonates till date with millions of people who read it, and is used by them as a guide in their day-to-day life.

At one level, as the super conscious energy behind the Bhagavad Gita, Krishna is the supreme Lord and God. At other levels, He is the beautiful and naughty child every mother loves to adore; the dashing graceful youth that every damsel dreams of being in love with; the perfect friend who one can turn to at any time of need; the sagacious counselor that kings and Saints seek advice from; Krishna is all this and more. Krishna is not a moral beacon as Rama or Balarama, as two of the other incarnations were, or the dispassionate Sage that Buddha was. Krishna was, is and will be human, so very easy to identify with, so easy to love, so easy to be devoted to.

Krishna has said in the scriptural Bhagavad Gita that He will take human form upon Earth from time to time. He declares:

To protect the good
To destroy the evil
To establish righteousness
I present myself age after age

In the case of these divine and popular incarnations of Vishnu that are part of the *Puranic* lore of Hindu mythology, we do not have historical proof of any one except Buddha. Krishna and Balarama are supposed to have lived 5000 years ago in the previous age of *Dwapara Yuga* and Rama lived much earlier in the *Satya Yuga (According to the Hindu calendar, there are four ages in all in each cycle of the Universe, and each age is many hundreds of thousands of years long. We are now in Kali Yuga – the fourth quarter of this cycle of the Universe.)* But then, hard evidence is difficult to come by so far.

In addition to these incarnations of mythology, there are many other historical beings who we know have walked the planet Earth, who are also revered as incarnations in the Hindu belief system. In recent times of historical recollection, Mahavira, the founder of the religion of Jainism, Adi Sankara, the Hindu reformer saint who propounded the concept of *advaita* - non duality, Chaitanya Mahaprabhu, a saint steeped in devotion to Lord Krishna, Ramakrishna *Paramahamsa*, an enlightened Master of recent times who lived near Calcutta, his disciple Vivekananda who spread his message overseas, Shirdi Saibaba, a saint of Muslim origin who was revered by Muslims and Hindus alike, Bhagwan Ramana Maharishi of Tiruvannamalai of whom we have spoken here earlier, are among many who have been considered as incarnations and revered in India.

Ramakrishna Paramahamsa tells us this story:

Three men were strolling aimlessly together, when they reached a garden surrounded by a high wall. One of them jumped over the wall and saw a beautiful orchard with many fruit trees. He jumped in without further ado to enjoy what the orchard had in store. He never even thought about telling his friends about what he saw; so focused he was upon his own pleasures; most of us are in this mode of living.

The second man then peeped over the wall. He too saw the bountiful orchard. He called out to his friend below, told him what he saw and jumped over to enjoy himself. He had no patience to wait for his friend, but decided to at least let his friend know about it. There are many preachers who are in this mode of living; they can talk and inform, but have no experience to share.

The third person looked over the wall and saw the fruit trees. He has known the experience of these fruits and knew how delicious they were. Instead of jumping over the wall to enjoy himself, he turned around, walked back to the village where he came from and told the entire community about the wondrous orchard and how to reach it.

Says Ramakrishna: ***This man is a true incarnation.***

Incarnations are beings who have seen the wonder of the ultimate spiritual Truth, experienced the bliss of the universal energy and have the freedom to stay on in that bliss forever and ever. Yet they come back to planet Earth to tell others about the glory of what they themselves have experienced. They are on a mission that Existence has sent them for, which they execute with the compassion that only an enlightened Master can possess; the compassion to make others see in their own selves, and in every other being, the divinity that lies.

In every generation, there are incarnations who descend on this Earth to show others the bliss that they themselves experience continually; their mission is to help all others reach the same bliss that they experience. It is this infinite compassion to the rest of the world without differentiation that sets an incarnation apart from other beings, however evolved they may be spiritually.

Nithyananda explains simply.

Take a clean white board. The white background is the universal energy. Draw circles on it with a blue marker pen. These circles represent the living beings; the blue lines you have drawn are the bodies. Now erase the circle. That is what happens at death. The body gets erased and the spirit merges back into the universal energy.

In the case of ordinary human beings, their desires, the *vasana*, creates a tinge inside the circle. It is then difficult for the spirit to merge into the background energy. The spirit leaving the body at death needs another body that is capable of fulfilling its carried over desires, the *vasana*.

In the case of enlightened Masters, they have no desires; they are of no mind state; they have no *vasana.* Their spirits, untinged by *vasana,* effortlessly merge into the universal energy. Whenever a need is felt in Planet Earth, the energy of the enlightened Masters is sent back to Earth with a mission to fulfill. These energies are the incarnations. Each incarnation has a mission as defined by the need expressed and as decided by Parasakti, the universal energy.

Uniqueness of each Incarnation

In Ramakrishna *Paramahamsa*'s biography by his disciple Saradananda, the biographer discusses why and how incarnations arrive upon planet Earth. Saradananda traces the origin of such incarnations to Vedic times when sages of divine consciousness started being revered as incarnations. In India, its spiritual legacy of the *Vedic* and *Puranic* times still lives on as a palpable energy. Its people accept and believe in the truth of conscious births of incarnations, who arrive fully enlightened upon planet Earth.

As Krishna proclaimed in the Gita, these incarnations arrive upon planet Earth with a clear mission. Existence, the Cosmic Energy, provides these incarnations the necessary energy to fulfill their mission in a choiceless manner. Each incarnation is unique and the mission of each incarnation is personalized.

Saradananda talks about various levels of spiritual evolution from within and outside of the definition of incarnations. He also tells us as to how these people can be identified, based on the natural characteristics they are endowed with from birth.

Each incarnation differs from the other in the way he performs his mission. Each one his own path, though the goal is the same. Their goal is to teach the rest of humanity that each one is divine and that all humans, with effort on their part, can be liberated into that divinity from bondages of the world. Each incarnation may express the same experience differently.

Incarnations are not miracle makers: Teleporting and Energy Healing are scientific

In the human form that they have assumed, these living incarnations are subject to the same physical laws of existence as all of us human beings are. It is easy to visualize and accept the divinity of a Krishna who none of us has seen. When we live around a living incarnation, however, whose physical functions are no different from ours, who we can see eating and sleeping, questions arise about the acceptance of their divinity by many.

It is easy for the average human to be impressed by what may be called supernatural feats of spiritual beings; very often these feats seem unbelievable, irrational and contradictory to all known laws of nature. Because we do not understand the laws of such feats such as teleportation or materialization of objects, we tend to classify them as miracles and consider those who perform such feats as divine beings. There are no miracles in nature; such miracles operate through natural laws that our scientists are yet to uncover and understand. And most certainly, these are not the scale of measure to identify and recognize incarnations.

In the case of materialization of objects, which is considered as an essential part of the tool kit of an enlightened Master by many Hindus, its underlying science is simple enough: No material is created in these 'miracles'; is material transported or teleported from one point to another. Matter dissolves into energy at one point and the energy that is teleported is reconverted into matter in the hands of one who is performing this 'miracle'. It is just the same way as voice is converted to digital waves when we speak on a mobile phone, which are again reconverted into voice at the receiver's phone. Telephony is understood; teleportation is yet to be understood; that's all. Those who perform these 'miracles' have acquired the skill to convert matter into energy and energy back into matter through their powers of meditation.

Tools of modern technology such as Kirlian photography which can capture energy can follow the path of a teleported object and show that there is no miracle involved here; just a feat whose scientific basis is yet to be understood.

Coming to energy healing, even a primary school student today is taught that there is intelligence residing in each cell of our body. Mind is not a vague entity that is to be found somewhere in the brain. It is a life force that is spread all over the body. Every part of our body is mind as well. Mind and body are not two separate terms; it should be mind-body.

When this is understood, spiritual or energy healing, viewed suspiciously by many, makes good sense. All illnesses are psychosomatic in one manner or another; these are caused by disturbances to the mind-body system in terms of energy blocks through emotional or physiological traumas; not to mind and body separately. Therefore healing the mind can cure the illness of the mind-body. Mind unlike body, as we understand body, is not matter; it is energy. Body and mind too, like matter and energy, are interchangeable and they are the same. Healing a sick person through energy healing of the mind seems unscientific only because this is not understood. It is very scientific if one understands recent advances in science.

Dr. Bruce Lipton describes his experiments at the single cell level in layman's terms in his milestone book Biology of Beliefs. In this book, he explains the mind-body behavior through the functionality of cells. Through a simple experiment with a single cell, he shows how the cell is attracted by nutrients so that it establishes itself in a growth mode and how it is repelled by toxins, when it sets itself up in a protection mode. He then goes on to show how the cell cannot at the same time be in a growth mode and a protective mode; it has to be in one or the other. Using this basic behavior, he logically shows how stress in today's world, repetitive and illogical, affects the mind-body, causing depression and leading to serious illnesses.

A spiritual healer who cures chronic and fatal diseases uses his energy at the cellular level to redress damage caused to the mind-body. His performance is miraculous only to the gullible; it is laughable only to those who do not understand the underlying science. When we understand the working of the cell at the molecular level as explained by scientists like Bruce Lipton, spiritual healing becomes extremely scientific and rational.

Fire walking is no miracle; there need be no hypnosis involved. With Nithyananda, many of us have walked over burning coal. All that we shed was the fear that fire would burn. When one walks over fire with wet feet, up to a reasonable distance, the conversion of water to steam takes care of the heat of the fire. There is scientific evidence to show that any one can walk on fire; all that we need to let go is our belief that fire will burn.

True incarnations go beyond the display of such seemingly extraordinary powers termed by us as miraculous because of our lack of understanding. Their mission is to help mankind, not to work miracles to impress other humans. Having experienced the divinity of their own beings, incarnations are focused on assisting the rest of mankind in experiencing the same divinity within them. Just the same way as a scientist develops formulae and techniques to reproduce phenomena of the outer world, mystics develop formulae and techniques to reproduce their own experiences of the inner world.

While a Master is able to apply these formulae so that others can experience what he has experienced, a true incarnation is able to transfer such experiences directly without the need for techniques or formulae. An incarnation liberates through his grace alone.

Over time in the Hindu tradition, great Masters have laid down the path and techniques to achieve liberation from the illusion that we are not divine. Patanjali, an enlightened Master, father of the yoga system and the greatest teacher ever, in his *Yoga Sutras,* specified a path of eight practices that leads to *yoga* or union, the union of the individual with the Divine. These eight practices: *yama* (5 virtues), *niyama* (5 rules of conduct), *asana* (sitting posture), *pranayama* (breathing), *pratyahara* (detachment from sensory inputs), *dharana* (focused consciousness), *dhyana* (meditation) and *samadhi* (state of being one with Existence), are valid today as techniques for spiritual evolution even after thousands of years.

Popular techniques of *yoga,* such as *asana* (yoga postures) and *pranayama* (breath control), which are now practiced worldwide, have their origin in Patanjali, whose mission in life was to share his wisdom in a practical manner with humanity at large.

Other great Masters communicated and communed differently. Ramakrishna *Paramahamsa* initiated his disciples into enlightenment by touching them. Ramana Maharishi liberated his disciples through silent communion. The concepts of *deeksha*, which is the initiation of the Master's grace to his disciple by sight, touch, and words are well documented in Hindu scriptures.

The greatest blessing that Existence can bestow upon a person is the opportunity to live with and around an incarnation, as his disciple. The Master, divine incarnate, just by his sheer presence can and will elevate one to enlightenment. Nothing else is needed but surrender to the Master. The mission of an incarnation is to lead other human beings to enlightenment.

Who is a Paramahamsa?

Hindu epics talk in wonder about a mythical bird that never touches the earth from birth to death. These birds soar high above the ground, far higher than any normal bird would. When this bird lays an egg, the egg hatches even as it falls to the ground. The fledgling infant bird starts flying as it comes out of the shell, still in mid air, and soars into the sky. When these birds die, they die while flying and they merge into space. Never once in its life does the bird touch ground.

These birds are called *Paramahamsa* or Supreme Swans. Ramakrishna, one of the greatest saints of modern India talks of these birds in adoration. Ramakrishna himself is aptly called *Paramahamsa*, a spirit who always soared without ever touching ground.

An enlightened being is called a *Paramahamsa*, when his spiritual awakening leading to enlightenment occurs before adolescence. Such a being never touches ground; his spirit soars high well before it is enmeshed in the web of worldly reality. *Paramahamsa* are rare beings whose innocent wisdom pierces even the most hardened heart and mind.

In such beings, the divine *kundalini* energy, which is the universal energy that flows through every individual, that is stored in the *muladhara chakra* (the energy center at the base of the spine) never moves downwards as it does with normal beings at adolescence. *Chakras* are virtual energy centers within our mind-body system that control our emotions and through this, influence our actions. There are seven major *chakras*, starting from the *muladhara* at the base of the spine to *sahasrara* at the crown of the head.

In all humans, this energy moves from upwards to downwards leading to sexual awakening and the desire to fulfill the need for procreation. In the case of the *Paramahamsa,* the *kundalini* energy is awakened before puberty and it moves upwards instead of downwards at the time of spiritual awakening, without causing any desire for sexual pleasure. The energy within the *Paramahamsa* stays pure, uncorrupted, and exceptional.

Paramahamsa are spirits who have realized the supreme and eternal truth of the Universe very early in life. Their purpose in life is to communicate to the rest of humanity this truth that has been gifted to them, in the hope that at least some others would glimpse this truth for themselves.

Each *Paramahamsa* communicates this message in his own inimitable style. Ramakrishna, forever, in divine ecstasy, inspired others through devotion or *bhakti.* Bhagwan Ramana Maharishi, another great *Paramahamsa,* communicated his message mainly in silence, through a process of discrimination or *viveka.* There are others who by their touch and at times by a mere glance, imparted their wisdom to disciples who were ready to receive the truth.

Even these great *Paramahamsa* had trouble convincing the rest of humanity to follow the path that they had traversed, and which they were keen to show to them. In his lifetime, Ramakrishna initiated about a dozen disciples into enlightenment, and it is only after his death through the efforts of his wife Sarada Devi and disciple Vivekananda, that his message spread worldwide.

During his lifetime, Ramana probably initiated a few more, not many more though. However, over time, their message spread, and more people were awakened to the possibility that they too had divinity in them. The mission of these Masters was not wasted. It is a continuum of enlightened Masters who serve this planet, each taking off from where the earlier Master had left. All *Paramahamsa* are one and the same energy, all performing the same mission with uniqueness that Existence has defined for them.

Why does a Paramahamsa need to struggle, when he is already enlightened?

Since *Paramahamsas* are realized beings, why then do they struggle and undergo intense penance in their lives in their pre-enlightenment period? The same question arises in our minds in the context of the life of Nithyananda. If he was enlightened from birth as an incarnation, the question may arise in our minds as to what was the need for him to go through such intense *tapas* (spiritual penance) by wandering on foot, eating minimal food, and enduring many a test. Why?

He says that there was no suffering involved in his case. Looking at him as an onlooker, we may feel he must have withstood great suffering and we may see his process of enlightenment as extremely difficult.

We need to understand that an incarnation appears on this earth fully enlightened. He has no qualities or attributes, called *guna* in Sanskrit, that define his behavior. The three *guna* or attributes with which we lead our lives are: *sattva guna* - the highest state of calmness and detachment denoting a state of spiritual evolution, *rajas* - a state of active aggression that is focused on achievement of material goals, and *tamas* - a state of inactive passivity, sloth and negativity that leads to ineffective functioning as an individual.

An enlightened being is beyond these three attributes. However, in order to function on earth, in the human body, he is infused with a little bit of *satvic* attribute. Over a period of time, through his own spiritual practices, he burns this *satvic guna* also off.

This *satvic* attribute is the incarnation's hangover of desires needed for action in this world that comes along with the spirit as it enters the body, termed as *prarabda karma*, even though the enlightened being has no carry over *vasana*, which is normally the basis for *prarabda karma.*

It is like this: You cannot make anything out of pure unalloyed 24 carat gold. It is too pure and too fragile to be of any practical purpose. So you need to alloy it with copper or some other impurity. That's the way it is with an incarnation, a *Paramahamsa.* He is born with some *satvic* attributes, as an alloying attribute, so that he can live and survive on this planet Earth.

Lives of all great incarnations follow a similar path. In almost all cases, these beings are born in a middle class environment; in not too luxurious a lifestyle that diverts their minds and in not too harsh an environment that limits their potential. By and large, these beings choose a parental environment conducive to their spiritual evolution. Their parents in most cases are of a religious bent of mind, though perhaps not fully open to the child taking to an ascetic life.

All incarnate beings grow up with an explicit interest in spiritual matters. They are devotional, they are very curious about spiritual truths even at an early age and go to great lengths to seek the mission they are sent down for. However, the consciousness of their own enlightened being seems to be hidden from them till the point of their re-enlightenment, so to speak, until the remainder of the *satvic guna* is also fully burnt off.

In a *Paramahamsa,* actions arise out of thoughts and desires spontaneously as seeds of desires (known as *bija karmas*) from their Causal energy layer. We all have seven layers of energy around our mind-body system. The first is the gross Physical body layer; the second is the Breath layer or *Pranic* layer; the third is the Mental or emotional layer; the fourth is the Etheric or Subtle layer that houses the energy centers that are the *chakras*; the fifth is the Causal body

layer, which once crossed by the spirit does not allow it to return to the body. The final two layers are the Cosmic and *Nirvanic* layers. The *Nirvanic* layer is the state that enlightened beings reach.
In ordinary humans, desires arise from the lower layers, from Physical to Etheric; some of these desires are carried over from previous births as *vasana* and most other desires are developed through actions during their present birth. By and large, desires that one is born with are one's natural desires for which one has been bestowed with all the energy to fulfill. That is why Mahavira, founder of the religious group of Jainism says, 'Every human being is born on this planet Earth with all that is needed to meet his needs; no one will be deprived of his needs if one trusts the Universe.'

Vasana is the mental attitude that creates desires, *samskara* are the developed desires that prompt fulfillment and *karma* are the actual deeds of action. We can liken *vasana* to a seed, *samskara* to a small plant and *karma* to a fully-grown tree, in their order of development. What is carried over from birth to rebirth through the process of death is the *vasana*, the mental attitude.

In an incarnation or *Paramahamsa,* no desires are carried over from previous births since at their enlightenment, in previous births, all their *karma, samskara* and *vasana* have all been dissolved.

Paramahamsa have none of these residual desires, memories, and actions, as all these, the *vasana*, *samskara* and *karma,* are destroyed at enlightenment. However, as we saw earlier, their beings are infused with some minimal desires at birth to allow them to be reborn in human form.

In a *Paramahamsa,* these desires infused at birth arise from the Causal layer, which is the transition point of no return for the spirit. The Causal layer is the state of coma, where the body can stay for long periods of time. Till the spirit does not leave this layer of energy, it has the option to return to the body. Near death experiences are based on the journey of the spirit up to this point.

These desires of *Paramahamsas* at their Causal energy level, the transition point, carry their own energy for fulfillment. Therefore, as soon as these desires and thoughts arise, they get fulfilled. As they are fulfilled, these thoughts drop completely; the desires die out; there is no hangover.

For instance, let us say a thought arises in a *Paramahamsa* to eat. That thought in him brings with it the energy. There is energy in his thought; the energy behind that thought brings in its own fulfillment of that thought or desire. He then eats. Then the thought disappears. Next, the thought arises to walk. He walks. That is how it was with nithyananda's wanderings, the *parivrajaka* and his spiritual penance, *tapas*. Thoughts and actions happened on their own, with the thoughts bringing their own energy for fulfillment and getting extinguished completely upon fulfillment.

Paramahamsa do not have borrowed and acquired desires. Their needs and desires are limited to the very basic needs that their beings have been sent with. That's why they stay pure. They have no attachment to material pleasures, as they come with the realization that all material and sensory pleasures are illusionary and impermanent. They neither seek, nor are they tempted, by these diversions. They merely witness what transpires around them and carry on.

During his wanderings and spiritual practices, nithyananda was just a witness to his thoughts and actions. He just watched as the thoughts came up to his mind-body and got fulfilled.

Imagine that you are used to eating at noon. Hunger appears at noon. Then you eat and let go the hunger. Your *samskara* gets fulfilled; it will be burnt out. Most often with us, thoughts are induced by others; desires are not our own, but borrowed from others. We eat because we are told to eat or because it is time to eat. Therefore, these thoughts and desires do not carry the energy needed for fulfillment. We partially fulfill these desires and they linger as a hangover.

In an enlightened being, only when the body really expresses hunger at the time of its need, this hunger is expressed as a desire for food; and as soon as this desire is expressed it is fulfilled. The food will appear from somewhere. The desire is inborn as a need; it is not a want that is created by the mind.

All our sufferings are due to this fact of created desires alone; of our inability to fulfill our desires; because our desires are not our own. This is what Buddha meant when he talked about the fact that desires lead to suffering. There are desires that we allow others to force upon us, and desires that we pick up from them unknowingly. Buddha was referring to those desires borne out of human greed and jealousy; desires that have nothing to do with one's needs but are covetous wants borne out of greed.

The entire *parivrajaka*, the wandering all across India was an inner journey for nithyananda. It was much less of an outer journey. He had traveled about 30,000 kilometers. If one had taken a train or bus, this distance could have been covered in a few months at the most. But he kept going up and down; north and south; east and west; he went forward and backtracked. He had no plan.

As the thought arose to walk to some place or go to some place, he went there by whatever means was available. If the thought was to take a train, he took a train. He never bought a ticket. He had no money. When he had left home, he had vowed not to touch money.

Once in a train near Kolkata (known earlier as Calcutta), a ticket examiner asked nithyananda for his ticket. In his practically non-existent Bengali language skill, mixed with broken Hindi, nithyananda asked him, 'What ticket? I am *Brahman* (the universal energy), you are *Brahman*, this train is *Brahman*, and the ticket is also *Brahman*. **Why then a ticket?!'**

The Master laughs uproariously when recalling the incident to us; everyone is in splits as he recalls himself asking the bewildered ticket examiner: Ki ticket? Aham brahman! Aap brahman! Gadi brahman! Parchi brahman! Ki ticket?

The ticket examiner was totally confused. However, he was a good man. He never asked him for the ticket again. In fact, he bought some food for him at the next station and gave it to him to eat.

Nithyananda says that in most of Northern India the saffron cloth is truly respected unlike in the South; people consider it a privilege and merit to feed and take care of the saffron clad. There is no logical argument that beggars could also wear the saffron cloth and could be fake ascetics. The attitude is: so what, if one is needy, and if we have the wherewithal, let us feed them. This is true charity that flows from the being, with no tangible expectation in return.

Purification of the Paramahamsa

During his *parivrajaka* days, nithyananda's body moved wherever his thoughts took him. The energy of his thoughts led him to action. There was never any un-fulfillment.

You may ask: What do you mean by un-fulfillment?

When what we desire is fulfilled completely, and when no traces of that desire linger unfulfilled, all the *samskara* associated with that desire and experience are dissolved or burnt out and eliminated. Nothing remains inside; no baggage; no left over desires; there is no hangover.
Imagine that your being is a bean bag. All the beans inside are the *bija karma,* seeds of desire and *vasana,* essence of mental attitudes. When they drop, the bag starts collapsing.

In our case, if we feel hungry, we eat without even being aware of what we eat. Most often we eat not because there is a need to eat or that the body is hungry, but because it is time to eat or because our friends or family want us to eat. The eating happens unconsciously, with no awareness, often without a need. It is no wonder that we feel tired after eating, whereas the energy of the food should make us vigorous.

When we do eat, we rarely focus on the eating. We do everything else; we talk; we watch TV; we read newspapers; if nothing else, we replay what we had done earlier on in the day in our mental screen. Whatever we eat, however much we eat, when we eat like this with no awareness, we remain unfulfilled. We keep eating without satisfaction, without fulfillment; without dissolving the *samskara*.

Practically every other activity that we indulge in happens this way. When we are in the execution of one activity, our mind is busy doing something else. Often we multitask, with no focus on any one activity.

An enlightened Zen Master was asked what the difference between him, an enlightened being, and an ordinary being is. He said simply, 'I eat when I eat; I sleep when I sleep. That is the difference.'

In nithyananda, the eating happened consciously, when the body needed sustenance. The thought arose as part of a body need and not because of other external stimuli. Our body is such a beautiful organism that it is able to perform many complex actions without even us being aware of these activities. Why does a body that can digest the food we eat without us being aware, need our attention to prompt it through external stimuli? We bring about this situation by ignoring our body, by remaining unconscious of its needs and forcing into it our desires borrowed from others. As a consequence we suffer.

However small they may be, even in an incarnation, there are still *samskara* or unfulfilled desires till enlightenment; the alloy element is still in the gold. At the point of enlightenment, these *samskara* burn off completely, leaving just pure gold behind.

You can see the difference in Nithyananda's photographs before and after enlightenment. Grace simply happened at enlightenment and it is visible.

Someone asked Nithyananda as to what would have happened had he resisted the thoughts as they arose in him. He said that the situation did not arise, as he seemed to have no choice.

The spirit of the witnessing consciousness within him led him to following the thoughts as they arose, and witnessing them as they were fulfilled. It was choicelessness. It was Existence which propelled his actions.

Chapter - 3

A *Paramahamsa* Appears

An Incarnation and a Paramahamsa is born in Tiruvannamalai: Story of a conscious birth

It was under the glow of the mighty mountain Arunachala and in the holy energy center reinforced by the *jyotirlingam* Arunachaleshwara, that nithyananda was born as the second child of Arunachalam and Lokanayaki.

Nithyananda says, remembering his conscious birth:

'It was neither dark nor light-filled; an indeterminate color covered planet Earth. Suddenly a bright and brilliant light appeared from a region, which I now see as Southern India. I entered into that light in the form of a brilliant meteor. The very next sight that I perceived with my inner eye was Arunachala, and I knew that I had assumed the body once more; I had entered the womb of my mother. It was a conscious birth. I entered into the body at 11:45 pm. I took a *muhurta*, which is a period of about 45 minutes in the Hindu system of time measurement, to settle into the body.'

nithyananda's mother discovered that she was with her second child when she was on a pilgrimage to the holy temple town of Tirupati. She was sick and when the doctor examined her, she was found to be pregnant. nithyananda's connection with Lord Venkateshwara at Tirupati, another form of Lord Vishnu, thus started well before his birth. His mother had actually wanted a daughter, as a second child since her first born was a boy, and was somewhat disappointed when the second child too, was a male child.

nithyananda was born on 1st January 1978 at 32 minutes past midnight in the holy town of Tiruvannamalai in South India.

He was named after his mother's father as Rajasekaran, as per the local custom. The name referred to Siva, and meant 'King of Gods'. nithyananda was born in the Tamil month of *Margazhi* (December-January). Lord Krishna refers to Himself as *Margazhi* amongst the months. It is the month of the *brahma muhurta* – the period of the *Devas*, (divine beings), their early morning, the holiest time of the day. It is the month in which many great sages and enlightened Masters have been born: Ramana Maharishi, J Krishnamurthi, Sharada Devi, Seshadri Swami, Vivekananda and many others. It is considered the holiest of the months.

Quantum Spirituality

nithyananda was born in Tiruvannamalai, on the *ashtami* day, the eighth day of the waxing moon. *Ashtami* is considered to be worldly and therefore not considered a favorable period by ascetics. Legend has it that *ashtami* prayed to Krishna to redeem itself and Krishna decided to be born on the *ashtami* day to prove to the world that spirituality can be pursued by a person of the world, while still leading a material life of comfort.

It is very much in this tradition of Krishna's philosophy that Nithyananda preaches today the concept of Quantum Spirituality where materialism and spirituality meet, seamlessly combining material success and spiritual evolution. There is no need to make a choice, Nithyananda says, between the normal life of material goals of family, career, money and success that one seeks and spiritual values of renunciation and perceiving the rest of the world to be one's own. This concept has changed the lives of many who have heard Nithyananda, by removing the feeling of the guilt of having to make such a choice.

This is a beautiful story from the epic Mahabharata, as told by the sage Markandeya to the Pandava Prince Yudhishtra:

There was once an ascetic named Kaushika who observed his vow of Brahmacharya, practice of celibacy in preparation for a spiritual life as a monk- with great steadfastness and devotion.

One day, he sat under a tree reciting the scriptures. A crane, perched on the top of the tree, defiled his head with its droppings. He looked up at it, and his angry look killed the bird and it fell down dead.

Kaushika was pained when he saw the dead bird lying on the ground.

He regretted that the evil thought that passed in his mind in a moment of anger had killed an innocent bird. A while later, he felt hungry and went to beg alms as usual in line with his spiritual discipline.

He stood before the door of a house to receive his food. The housewife was cleaning utensils at that time. Kaushika waited in the hope that she would attend to him after her work was over.

In the meantime, the master of the house returned, tired and hungry, and the wife had to attend to his needs, wash and dry his feet and serve him food.

Kaushika thought she had forgotten him waiting outside. However, after attending to her husband, she came out with alms to give him.

She said, 'I am sorry to have kept you waiting long. Pardon me.'

Kaushika got irritated and said, 'Lady, you have made me wait for such a long time. This indifference is not fair.'

The woman told Kaushika, 'Kindly do forgive me. I was serving my husband and hence the delay.'

Kaushika remarked, 'It is right and proper to attend on the husband, but the sanyasi also should not be disregarded. You seem an arrogant woman.'

She said, 'Be not angry with me and remember that I kept you waiting only because I was dutifully serving my husband. I am no crane to be killed by a violent thought, and your rage can do no harm to the woman who devotes herself to the service of her husband.'

Kaushika was taken aback. He wondered how the woman knew of the crane incident.

She continued, 'Brahmachari (celibate monk), you do not know the secret of duty, and you are also not aware that anger is the greatest enemy that dwells in man. Forgive the delay in attending to you. Go to Mithila and be instructed in the secret of good life by Dharmavyadha living in that city.'

Kaushika was amazed. He said, 'I deserve your just admonition and it will do me good. May all good come to you'.

With these words he went to Mithila.

Kaushika reached Mithila and looked for Dharmavyadha's residence, which he thought would be some lonely hermitage far from the noise and bustle of common life.

He walked along magnificent roads between beautiful houses and gardens in that great city and finally reached a butcher's shop, where a man was selling meat. His amazement was great when he learnt that this man was Dharmavyadha.

Kaushika was shocked beyond measure and stood at a distance in disgust. The butcher suddenly rose from his seat, came to him and inquired, 'Revered sir, are you well? Did that chaste lady send you to me?'

Kaushika was stupefied.

'Revered sir, I know why you have come. Let us go home,' said the butcher and took Kaushika to his house where Kaushika saw a happy family and was greatly struck by the devotion with which the butcher served his parents.

Kaushika took his lessons from that butcher on dharma, man's calling and duty. Afterwards, he returned to his house and began to tend his parents, a duty that he had neglected before.

Vyadha Gita, the teachings of the butcher to the *brahmachari,* explains how by leading a normal life of a householder, one can still achieve liberation.

Portents of the future

In *Bhagavatam*, one of the great epics of Hindu mythology, before he begins, sage Vyasa says to Krishna: Before starting your story, the story of the Divine, who else can I remember but You! In the same light, as we begin this story, the story of an incarnation, let us remember the Energy that landed as Nithyananda upon this planet.

When talking to us, the Master once said, 'When I talk about my birth and life, I do not know at all how I am going to express myself. I do not know how IT is going to express Itself. I too can only bow down to that energy and along with you all, allow that Energy to work the way It wants to.'

The birth the Master said was conscious and wonderful. There was no separate experience, experiencer, or experienced; it was all one. There was no duality; the experience was like darkness covered by darkness, light covered by light. It was pure Consciousness; it was live energy. It was pure awareness, *sat chit ananda.* Pure Consciousness is such; it must be such. It is alive (*sat*), It knows It is alive (*chit*), and it is in bliss being alive (*ananda*); such is *satchitananda.*

Nithyananda had talked in this context of His experience with a *naga sadhu* in Uttar Kashi during his *parivrajaka,* the wandering days as an ascetic. This *sadhu* never said anything. nithyananda kept asking the *sadhu* to teach him something, but the older man never opened his mouth. One day the *sadhu* made preparations to leave. nithyananda asked him for permission to accompany him. The *sadhu* signaled 'no'. He gave the pipe that he used to smoke with to the young man. nithyananda said, 'The pipe might get lost, but your words will be remembered, please say something. Whatever you say I shall treat as a *mantra*, as a chant, even if you call me a fool!'

The *sadhu* then said, '*deham naham, koham soham*' and began to leave.

This meant, 'I am not the body; who am I? I am Whole.'

nithyananda took this as a blessing. He said to the *sadhu*, 'Please explain what you mean, I need to digest and internalize what you have said.'

The *sadhu* gave the young man a blow with his fire tongs and said, 'That's why I never said anything before. If I say one word you will ask for more, like you are doing now.'
Suddenly it dawned on nithyananda that he was alive, he knew he was alive, he was enjoying being alive; he understood the meaning of *satchitananda*. *Satchitananda* is *samadhi* state, when there is awareness; not just *sat*, truth of being alive, but *chit*, the knowledge of being alive, and *ananda*, the bliss of being alive. Even in deep sleep, we are alive, we are in *sat*; but unlike in *samadhi*, we are not in *chit* and *ananda*, at the same time.

Nithyananda described his birth process as a sequence of three scenes, of three *kshana* (a measure of time). The first scene was one of perceiving a light, a flame that emanated from some place in South India. The second scene was himself, the energy, floating into that light. The third scene was conscious awareness of Arunachala, the place, the mountain, and the deity at Tiruvannamalai. He knew he had arrived.

When a spirit leaves one body for another, it has three *kshana* to find another body. The spirit enters the new body just three *kshana* before the body enters the world; three *kshana* before it leaves its mother. Till that point in time, the body of the infant is part of the mother's life energy; it has no life energy of its own.

These three *kshana* are the three scenes described by Nithyananda as the scenes before his birth. *Kshana* in the Hindu concept of time is not chronological, measured by movement of a pendulum. *Kshana* is the time between two thoughts and varies individually based on state of mind.

The spirit chooses a body based on its past *samskara.* In the case of enlightened beings who have no residual *samskara*, it is Existence, *Parasakti*, that decides where they go. In the case of all those who are with *samskara*, it is the past *samskara*, the embedded memories, and the *vasana*, the mindset borne out of these *samskara*, that decide the next body, the next set of parents, the next location and the next life. The new body is borne with its *prarabda karma*, the inbuilt driving force, which is the carry over of its past *vasana*.

The memory of the *vasana* is lost as the spirit leaves the body through the Causal layer of energy, when it goes into coma; the spirit, the purpose with which it has left its earlier abode. It forgets its *prarabda karma.* Conscious Birth enables this memory to be retained; it enables one to remember the purpose of one's present life. When the *prarabda* is remembered, it is possible to change it; all one requires is the awareness.

They say Buddha walked when He was born. What they mean is that He was aware the moment He was born. He was aware of his *prarabda karma.* So was Nithyananda. Nithyananda has said that He is working on techniques to enable the process of Conscious Birth.

As we saw earlier, baby nithyananda was born at 12:30 am, exactly 45 minutes after he entered the body in his mother's womb, on the First of January 1978, on New Year's day. He was born on the star or *nakshatra* of *chitra*, the 'shining' star, on the eighteenth day of the Tamil *Margazhi* month, on the eighth *ashtami* day of the waning moon, the same as Lord Krishna. The number eighteen has always been auspicious in the Hindu calculations. The Bhagavad Gita has 18 chapters as also a number of other scriptural works.

When such an auspicious energy enters the Earth, Earth celebrates, the whole Existence celebrates. That's why they say that when Krishna was born, the Gods and Goddesses showered blessings and danced in celebration. At Nithyananda's birth, the whole world celebrates each year, as it is New Year's Day!

It is as if a hole is drilled in the Collective Consciousness layer for this Energy to land. When there is such an opening, it also can be used to move back into Collective Consciousness. That's why a Master's birthday is auspicious, and is celebrated as *Jayanthi*, which means: He came, He visited this Planet, He is going. Meditating upon the Master's formless energy on this auspicious day, gives one a chance to have a glimpse of the Collective Consciousness.

Within forty-five minutes or two *muhurta*, nithyananda was fully aware of being in his body. He was conscious of all that was happening around him. He felt it as a joyful experience.

I asked nithyananda's mother about the delivery. She smiled and said, 'he was a big baby, but it was an easy and painless delivery.'

Exactly 22 years after nithyananda entered his body on this planet, he would reach enlightenment, severing the thin line that held him to the planet. During these 22 years, he was visiting people on this planet in a relaxed and conscious way. He was gradually shedding the little *satvic* guna that he came to be born with through the *tapas* (penance) and *parivrajaka* (wandering) that Existence had ordained for him.

nithyananda was born in the community of Saiva Vellalars, a community of religious people in Tamil Nadu. People from this community used four different caste titles, such as Nayanar, Chettiar, Mudaliar, and Pillaimar. While going through His family tree with Nithyananda, we sometimes found it confusing that different ancestors had different caste titles. Moreover, these caste titles used by Saiva Vellalars was also used, sometimes more commonly, by other caste groups,

According to his parents, their second baby never cried at birth; its spirit was so relaxed and comfortable; the Doctor had to tap the baby to make sure that it was alive! There was no pain in the birth to the Being. Based on the mother's weight and size, the Doctor expected twins, and the baby justified it at 10 pounds!

The child was born in *Kanya rasi* and *Kanya lagnam* (moon and sun signs of Virgo), normally indicative of a female child. When the family priest drew up the baby's horoscope, he found that the stars and planets had aligned themselves in an exceptional manner that he had never seen before as an astrologer. After extensive study and consultation to ensure that he was not making a mistake, the priest declared to the startled parents that the baby would grow up to be a *raja sanyasi* or a 'king amongst holy men'. The priest considered himself blessed to have been able to cast the child's horoscope, and stopped practicing astrology after foretelling the baby's future.

nithyananda's parents were not very happy with this prediction. However much a family may respect saints and revere holy men, no parents want their own child to become a monk; so too it was with nithyananda's parents. They had no desire to see their son turn into a monk, renouncing the material world. Like all other normal parents, they too wanted the propagation of their family through the progeny of their children and were quite upset to learn that this might not happen.

They wanted to know from the priest if such an eventuality of the boy becoming a *sanyasi* could be prevented through ritualistic and religious interventions. The priest confessed that he knew of no method to prevent his prediction from coming true. He however suggested that they keep this knowledge away from the child in the hope of postponing the inevitable.

Many years earlier, nithyananda's great grandfather Kumaraswami Chettiar had met an enlightened Master and had a spiritual experience. When this man decided to give up his material way of living, he threw out all his belongings, including jewelry, from his house on to the street so that any passer by could pick them up and walk away. He went away from home and lived near a cremation ground, Bhoomandakolam in Tiruvannamalai. Later he traveled to Varanasi on a pilgrimage and passed away there.

A wandering mendicant once came to Kumaraswami's household seeking alms. As the lady of the house was about to come out with food to serve the ascetic, someone from inside shouted out sarcastically that able-bodied people should work and earn, and not beg. The holy man walked away without accepting the food that was offered to him, saying as he left, that in that household, at least one person in each generation would end up begging.

nithyananda's very birth removed that curse laid on his family several generations earlier by that wandering *sanyasi*. It is said that an enlightened Master's birth removes the *karma* of his ancestors and progeny for seven generations each way.

Kumaraswami Chettiar's wife used to call nithyananda an incarnation of Kumaraswami himself. Kumaraswami used to wear a big *rudraksh mala* with the *kandi*, which was a family tradition, symbolizing great spirituality. Nithyananda says that this man lived like a *Paramahamsa*, a realized soul, and that was why he could walk away from all his wealth without a thought. Kumaraswami's daughter, Dhanakoti Ammal, used to call nithyananda *Jnana Pandita*, a wise scholar.

Conscious birth of Incarnations

Early one chilly morning, during the fall of 2005, a group of us sat at the feet of the Master at the newly opened ashram at Duarte, near Los Angeles, USA.
He spoke to us on the background to His conscious birth.

When a pup or even a baby is born, it takes time for the newborn to settle into its body and perform. In fact, a human child takes longer than any other animal to move or walk. A pup or a calf struggles after it is born for a few minutes, gets up tentatively, wobbles around and is functional almost immediately. A human child, however, takes several months before it starts moving.

It happens the same way with the human spirit as well. To evolve and get liberated, the human spirit struggles through its *samskara*.

Samskara, as we saw earlier, are the collection of the embedded impressions and memories of past actions and desires, both from this and previous births. From childhood, from the time we are in our mother's womb, we collect experiences and memories of experiences. Some of these memories carry through past births. These memories, *samskara*, are stored without our conscious knowledge in our mind-body system. These *samskara* drive our decisions, very often unconsciously.

In the normal course of events, most of us are bound by our *samskara* and live our entire life chasing them, forever unfulfilled. When experienced, but still unfulfilled, these *samskara* which are stored deep in our unconscious mind reappear with renewed vigor. Many of these *samskara* follow us through many birth cycles as mindsets and attitudes. A few amongst us, a few lucky ones, who are mostly guided by enlightened Masters, may find ways to work our way out of the bondage of our *samskara* through meditation, and sometimes through sheer devotion, and finally find liberation.

These few lucky beings are born with a burning desire to be enlightened. They have not been enlightened in previous births, have been close to it, have been close to enlightened Masters, but for one reason or another have missed the bus, so to speak. Such rare beings, who seek desperately in this birth and finally find liberation, enlightenment, *mukti*, *moksha* or whatever name you wish to give to this experience of being one with the Divine, the Cosmic Energy, Existence, are the *jeevan muktas* – the liberated souls.

Jeevan mukta is different from an incarnation. A *jeevan mukta* does not have a conscious birth; he is born like all of us and struggles through life in the same manner. He does not arrive on this planet Earth fully conscious of his true divine reality. He too practices *sadhana* (spiritual pursuits) diligently till his chosen path of *jnana* (wisdom, also spelt *gyana or gnana*), *bhakti* (devotion) or *dhyana* (meditation) leads him to the realization of his innate divinity.

Then, there are incarnations. Incarnations take birth consciously, fully aware of their divinity within. They too, may go through *sadhana* or spiritual pursuits; however, these pursuits in the case of incarnations arise out of the realization of their own divinity, instead of being the necessary prerequisite to such understanding and realization. The *sadhana* is part of their witnessing consciousness; part of the journey they are on without any definition of destination.

What we need to understand is this: Incarnations are already enlightened beings, who have descended upon planet Earth with a mission defined by the cosmic energy. They have no choice in this matter. It is as if the energy of these enlightened beings is sucked into Earth due to a combination of circumstances, wherein the cosmic energy decides that the presence of the energy of this enlightened being would be of value to human beings.

Incarnations are like the legendary swan, the *Paramahamsa*. These birds have conscious birth. *Paramahamsa* are incarnations, who come down to planet Earth fully realized, fully aware and conscious, and ready to fly fully conscious.

Jeevan mukta on the other hand are like pups, calves and infants who struggle to get up and move. Unlike other pups, calves and humans, *jeevan mukta* eventually learn to fly and reach the same level of realization as the *Paramahamsa.* At the level of divine realization, both *jeevan mukta* and *Paramahamsa* reach the same level; there is no difference in the level of enlightenment. The difference between them is the starting point, which is the conscious birth of the *Paramahamsa. Paramahamsa* do not need *sadhana* (spiritual practices) and *tapas* (penance) to reach enlightenment; they already are enlightened at birth. Their *sadhana* and *tapas* are only to inspire others and provide other spiritual *sadhaka* (spiritual practitioners) the template for guidance in their individual paths to enlightenment. You may be tempted to ask how we know whether we are dogs or Swans.

When this question was asked of him, Nithyananda said, 'If you are already a Swan, you will not find the need to be here. You must be at least a dog to be here! Otherwise you would not have reached this far and ask. If you are a Swan you would not even ask; you will simply know!'

Nithyananda Avatar

Those of us who have had the great fortune to come in contact with Nithyananda consider this event to be the greatest blessing that we have had in our lives. It is not any kind of intellectual analysis that has led us to our unflinching conviction that He is an incarnation, an *avatar*. He is as close to a *Poornavatar* as Krishna was, as would be possible.

There have been other enlightened Masters, who are rightly revered as incarnations. They all generated one or another aspect of the five great *bhava* (relationships) that attracted disciples to them; *dasa bhava*, the master-servant relationship as with Lord Rama and Hanuman; *vatsalya bhava*, mother-child relationship as between Yashoda and Lord Krishna; *matru bhava*, child-mother relationship as between Ramakrishna *Paramahamsa* and Mother Kali; *sakya bhava*, friendship as between Kuchela or Arjuna and Krishna; finally *madhura bhava*, the relationship of the beloved that Meera and Andal exhibited uninhibitedly towards Krishna.

The relationship that Nithyananda generates as the *Poornavatar,* Krishna did in the *Maha Bhava*, the relationship that combines many or all of these five *bhava* relationships. We have seen Him be a lovable Krishna at one time, an austere Siva at another, a loving Devi at another time, and a multi faceted Vishnu CEO at other times!

It is impossible to frame Him. 'To frame me,' He says, 'to capture me in one aspect is to convert me into a dead Master. I am alive, He says, and I change every moment.'

The only certainty that one can be of this Master is the uncertainty.

As He says time and again, 'Can you predict which way the river Ganga will flow? Where she will move next? She is *nature*, so am I;

I flow with the universe; I have no idea what I will do next; *Parasakti* decides that; not this body.'

Time and again we have stood in front of this Force of Nature, just watching, absorbing, imbibing, wondering, loving, completely overcome by gratitude for the sheer blessing that we have received to be in front of Him.

Why do Hindus worship idols?

Indian mythology refers to 330 million Gods; perhaps even 3.3 billion Gods. Hindus take these numbers in their stride. To most people unfamiliar with the Hindu philosophy, these numbers are reason for confusion, if not scorn and laughter.

Whatever follows in this chapter is not an endorsement of the Hindu religion. It is appropriate that the Western or Eastern reader, who is unfamiliar with certain aspects of the Hindu religion, is explained the background, making it easier to relate it to certain aspects of Nithyananda that were influenced strongly by the environment of his upbringing.

Nithyananda was brought up as a Hindu, in a conservative middle class joint family in a small town in Tiruvannamalai, in rural South India. Many of his early childhood experiences were related to this environment. It would be easier to relate with these experiences that influenced him, if we are familiar with the relevant aspects of the Hindu religion.

The explanation of Hindu religious practices here is in no way meant to be a criticism of any other religion or philosophy. Each religion evolved around a civilization, culture and philosophy and flourished based on the environment of its origin. When one understands and imbibes true spirituality, this understanding leads to a better understanding of the core of one's own religion through a process of inner awareness, and brings us to the conclusion that the core remains the same in all authentic religions.

There are religions and cultures that worship idols and there are religions that abhor idol worship. There are religions that condemn idol worship, associate idols with pagan worship and uncivilized behavior, and consider their own mode of formless worship as a more civilized and superior alternative. This probably happened as a result of inappropriate practices that emanated from rituals associated with idol worship, such as sacrifices of living beings etc.

Many of these practices stemmed from societal compulsions and the need to build power bases for religious leaders, rather than any deep understanding of a religious philosophy. Reformers, who were appalled at what they perceived to be negative in such ritualistic approaches, condemned not only the rituals but also the background from which these rituals originated. Unfortunately, these new religions too built their own form of rituals arising out of compulsions to control and direct. The chain of reformation, therefore, continues.
Then there are those cultures and religions, which are exclusive and bounded, who do not allow all those who do not accept their value systems in totality into their fold and forms of worship. We often hear followers of such religions say that if one does not believe in totality what their leaders and scriptures say, one is then in fact outcaste of their religion and possibly perceived as an enemy of the religious group.

Hinduism is an inclusive religion, open to all who walk in; there is no exclusivity of beliefs in the Hindu philosophy. Hindu philosophy allows dissent from within. *Sanatana Dharma,* the original scriptural name for Hinduism, means the 'eternal path of righteousness'. Hinduism is a journey of inclusive acceptance, not a destination of exclusive belief.

Belief systems that have been embedded in our unconscious from childhood block us from anything new and different that is in seeming contradiction to existing beliefs. Human beings limit themselves by such beliefs. Many of these beliefs are through societal and religious sanctions that are quite selfish in protecting the interests of those who control society and religion.

Such beliefs, imposed on us by society and religion, have no spiritual validity; there is no spiritual truth that underpins these beliefs. Truth has to be experienced in our inner most being with awareness; truth cannot be an instruction that can be imposed on us by anyone claiming to act on behalf of God. Any one who does that either as a religious leader or a social leader is acting out of his own self-interest, not of the interests of the believer.

All it requires is a little bit of introspection and intelligence from the human mind to become aware and conscious of the over arching truths which may seem to defy factual reality.

However, for the average human being, it is a complex and difficult task to contemplate upon the formless existential energy. It is too abstract, too distant; it is too much of an intellectual exercise; or alternatively, it requires blind faith, without understanding, to accept this concept. It is a lot easier for the average human to visualize this formless energy in easily identifiable superhuman forms, and to relate to such forms with devotion and emotion. This is the idea behind idol worship.

This is what Hindus did. They created forms to represent the formless to reach the masses; to link intellect with emotion; the head with the heart. Emotion is always stronger than intellect. They created forms that had features similar to humans and sometimes animals, which were familiar to them, forms with which they could easily identify and they made these forms, objects of worship, instilled with the divine energy. They worshipped the energy behind these forms, not the forms themselves. Mythology and folklore were created around these energy forms, once again to reach the masses.

There is little point in trying to reach with dry intellect, that which needs the heart to experience. Intellect without heart only creates monsters. Modern day terrorism is an outcome of intellect without emotion, head without heart.

Most Indians and almost all Hindus are familiar with the many forms that Hindu Gods (and Goddesses) take. Almost all Hindu households will have a *puja* room or an altar that holds pictures and idols of these many forms of divinity, as well as sages and enlightened Masters.

When Hindus worship idols of Gods and Goddesses, they do not worship stone, metal or wooden idols; what they worship are the visualized forms of the formless energy. What Hindus worship is the formless energy beyond the forms of these idols through the stone or wooden or metal idols.

Hindus worship the formless through the form. Worship is *through* the idol, never *of* the idol.

This concept of idol worship is one of the most misunderstood ideologies of Hindu religion, and it arises even amongst educated Hindus out of lack of knowledge of the underlying principle. It is far better to identify with a form of your visualization that appeals to you and which can uplift you, than to pray to the formless using one's dry intellect.
What the heart can reach, the head never can; only when you reach at least the heart level, the connection with the Being can begin.

Often times one is told by a well read, Western style convent or public school educated Indian, that he believes he is above all rituals including idolatry, and considers that it is foolish to worship a stone image.

If one has understood the concept of the formless energy behind the idols and has graduated to other ways of connecting with the formless energy, it is alright. But, without understanding the concept behind worship through idols, it is not becoming to condemn it.

We are all divine. We are all part of the universal energy.

Hindu philosophy believes that all living beings are divine in origin and in character. All religions, all great religions established by enlightened Masters say the same thing: We human beings are all divine in nature. There is absolutely no confusion on this score.

In Hinduism, this truth is clearly defined as divinity present in the individual, the soul, spirit or *atman.* Great declarations like *Tat tvam asi,* called *Maha Vakya*, found in Hindu scriptures means: Thou art That; you are Divine. There is no doubt whatsoever.

This divinity of the individual being is a holographic part of the divinity of Existence, of the Universe, of God, of the Cosmic Energy, of *Brahman* and of whatever else the name we wish to call that intelligent energy of creation.

Atman and *Brahman* are one and the same; God and Man are one and the same; they are the same energy. There is no room for an atheist belief in Hindu philosophy. There is no God outside of you; you *are* God. All that is needed is to understand and realize this Truth. Enlightened Masters have realized it; others have yet to. That is all the difference there is. The only barrier to this realization that we are one with divinity is our mind and belief systems.
Both *Atman* and *Brahman* are formless. They are energy. *Atman* is the energy enshrined in our mind bodies; *Brahman* is the Energy that pervades the Universe.

All that Hindu mythology states, based on this belief, is that every one of us is divinity, a deity, a God; not just the human beings but all living beings as well. The numbers of 330 million or 3.3 billion or 33 billion would refer to the number of beings on this planet Earth, at a given point in time. All these beings are forms of energy and are an integral part of the cosmic or universal energy.

The Hindu scriptures, the *Vedas* and the *Upanishad,* state very clearly that Existence is formless energy. It is formless both at the universal level and at the individual level. This energy is eternal, omniscient, omnipotent, and all pervading.

In the timeless Hindu scripture - the *Bhagavad Gita,* Krishna as the embodiment of the cosmic energy, says about this formless energy as it manifests itself within each one of us: No weapon can destroy this energy; water cannot wet It; wind cannot dry It; fire cannot burn It; It is eternal; It lives on.

What is implied here is that this energy, whatever we may call it, spirit or soul, lives on after the body is destroyed. Nithyananda described this beautifully on a piece of paper when he was asked what happens to the energy within when it leaves the body. He drew circles on the paper with a pen and said: See, the outline periphery of the circles that I have drawn is the body within which the energy is captured. The area within the circles is the energy of the living being. The white paper background, outside the circle outline is the universal energy from which we all arise and to which we return. When the energy leaves the body, the perimeters of the circles disappear and the space within the circle merges with the space outside the circle. There are no barriers any more. That is all.

Truly beautifully and simply described!

How can the concept of God become a reality?

God to most of us is a concept, not a reality. We attribute to Godhood what we perceive should be the attributes that we, as humans lack. When events do not go the way we wish them to, we immediately reject Godhood, rather than accept and surrender. True devotion, which is acceptance of life as it is, and one's surrender to the cosmic energy, can and will lead to realization of God as reality. This can happen perhaps more easily through worship of form and through rituals of devotion, as long as one is aware of the truth that the form is a representation of the formless energy. Often, it is difficult for the intellect to comprehend this.

Spirituality is beyond science, far beyond science. Einstein, arguably the greatest scientist who ever lived said, 'Where science ends, spirituality starts.' There is no proven scientific explanation till date for creation of the universe. There are hundreds of unproven hypotheses; the big bang theory, the primordial soup theory, the creation by aliens theory and so on; but none has either facts to support it or scientific evidence to prove it.

Spirituality states that the universe always existed and will continue to exist. Apart from Darwin and the Christian doctrines, which again are hypotheses without substantial proof, there is no proof as to how living matter emerged out of energy, what science terms as 'abiogenesis'. There is only this word in scientific lore, with no knowledge behind it.

Science, as in quantum physics, has established beyond a doubt that all matter is energy. The first verse of the first Upanishad, the great Hindu scripture, says beautifully: *Isa vasyam idam sarvam.* From Energy arises all matter. This was stated more than 5000 years ahead of Einstein. This is what Einstein referred to when he said, 'Where science ends, spirituality starts.'

He said, 'My theory could only talk about how all matter releases energy. Thousands of years ago there was wisdom that stated that all this matter came from a source of energy.'

If one looks deeper and deeper into any matter, as with looking at an atom through a highly powered electron microscope, all that we would find is emptiness. The emperor has no clothes! The atom has nothing to it! Energy is formless. Yet, we see things around us, which are in form.

It is not difficult for any one today, truly educated in science, to realize that ultimately form is formless, and that the formless can and is represented by form. This is what the great *rishis*, Hindu sages said many thousands of years ago. This is the basis for idol worship.

Chapter - 4

A growing Consciousness

Growing up in spirituality

As a baby, nithyananda was carried by his mother's father, Rajasekaran or Raju Mudaliar, whose name he had been given, to the Arunachaleshwara temple every day. His grandfather used to tell him mythological stories and legends of the Hindu tradition called the *puranas*, as they went around the temple.

Especially interesting to the child nithyananda were the stories of Prahlad, Dhruv and Markandeya. In Hindu *puranas,* Prahlad, Dhruv and Markandeya were from childhood, deeply attracted to spirituality. They spent all their time meditating upon forms of the divine and reached enlightenment before adolescence. They are venerated in Hindu legends as great sages; Dhruv, for instance, is considered to be the Pole Star, forever positioned in a distinguished fashion. Young nithyananda simply adored the valor of Markandeya or the devotion of Prahlad or the uniqueness that Dhruv beheld.

These stories were deeply imprinted in the child's memory. These mythical and mystical models became role models, inspiring him in his future activities. nithyananda's grandfather was his first teacher; and the stories that he heard from his grandfather were his first enjoyable lessons in spirituality.

From childhood, nithyananda's spiritual inclinations were very clear. An incident, very early in his life even before he was three, illustrates this: His grandmother, Dhanakoti Ammal, was very fond of her grandson. One day she wanted to give him a gift. So she opened up her box of jewelry to young nithyananda one day and asked him to pick whatever he liked. The young child without hesitation picked up a *rudraksh mala,* much to his grandmother's surprise.

Rudraksh mala is a necklace made of beads of plant seeds, which are usually worn by spiritually evolved people and those aspiring to the spiritual path. *Rudraksh* literally means Siva's tears and comes in many forms, depending on the number of facets the seed has. *Rudraksh* serves as a battery, getting charged by the energy produced during meditation, and discharging it as needed to the wearer. Any normal child would have picked up a bauble that shone; something that was visually attractive; nithyananda however, unerringly chose the *rudraksh* necklace.

As a child, nithyananda loved playing with images and idols of Gods and Goddesses, unlike other children who played with toys and dolls. He collected these idols and by associating with sculptors in the temple, learnt how to make them well, from wood, soft stone and wet earth. Some of the idols that he had made and worshipped and played with, are now on display at the ashram in Bangalore, India.

An instant *puja* room

At home, if the famous 'yellow bag' was missing from its place, it went without saying that nithyananda had taken it. Once school closed for holidays, nithyananda would gather his few friends and visit the temples and temple ponds in the neighborhood with the yellow bag on his shoulder. In these jaunts, he would do two things: one, he would ardently pick up every bit of trash he could sight in the vicinity of the temple and put in the garbage can, thus deeply satisfying his urge to keep the Lord's place clean; second: he would fill the 'yellow bag' with lots of wet earth. Back at home, he would make out of the wet earth, beautiful forms of the idols that he saw at the temples and decorate them with adoration and reverence.

Soon, he had a problem as to where to store the idols that were growing in number. No sooner than this thought occurred to him, a separate *puja* room took shape in his mind. nithyananda never compromised in realizing his spiritual urges. He had no money or material of his own to have a *puja* room for himself. He did not feel like asking for a separate room. As he sat in helpless contemplation, his eyes fell on a couple of biscuit tins. Instantly he knew what had to be done. With a hammer and chisel, a couple of long screws and small pieces of wood, he flattened the tins and made a small altar for his idols in the rear of his house.

Working through zest and spontaneity, seamlessly, he invited his friends and family members to his altar, offered *puja* to the idols and distributed puffed rice to them. A fleeting thought of an altar became a full-fledged reality in no time. To give shape to an altar and have a small function with a group of people would be an arduous task for someone his age; for young nithyananda, it was just another natural and joyful expression of his deep yearning for God.

Before or after attaining inner bliss, this aspect remained unchanged in him. Today, Nithyananda gathers people from world over, just by the power of thought, at the ashram or elsewhere, and conducts grand functions, radiating bliss to one and all.

In his altar, he would offer regular *puja* with great sincerity everyday. One day, his father missed his *dhoti* (white piece of clothing that Indian men wear) that he had put out on the clothesline to dry. He searched all over the house for it. As he passed by nithyananda seated at his altar, he caught the young boy using the *dhoti* in three pieces – one square piece as a floor mat, one around his waist and the third as a base for the idols. He along with nithyananda's mother watched with great awe, the boy's undaunted spiritual fervor. Nithyananda recalls today how his father never ever questioned him for time and again using his brand new and used *dhotis* for his various spiritual practices.

Another of nithyananda's favourites was a pair of wooden sandals. He had with him, a pair of wooden sandals called *paduka*, usually worn by ascetics. He would wear these all the time wherever he went, whether to temple festivals or to relatives, continuously making an infernal noise that every body else disliked!

At home one day, one of the family members had bought an aluminum vessel for an unduly high price. nithyananda's father was upset at the purchase and asked, 'Why this useless vessel for this much money?' nithyananda asked him if it was a useless vessel and he said 'yes' and walked away. The next day, as his father walked into the house, nithyananda went up to him excitedly holding an idol of Goddess Lakshmi. His father exclaimed, 'This is beautiful. Where did you get this from?' The boy replied, 'I made the useless thing into this useful thing.' The father could not understand and asked what he meant. He explained, 'You said that the aluminum vessel was useless, so I sold it at the shop down the road and bought this idol! Isn't that alright?' His father could not help but laugh and agree with the child's consistent and growing spiritual inclinations.

Book fair in Tiruvannamalai

At the town of Tiruvannamalai, there was once a book fair. nithyananda's maternal grandfather Raju Mudaliar, who had great interest in spiritual books, took young nithyananda with him and set out for the book fair. He sat him down near a bookstall with the stall owner, and went his way to look at books.

No sooner did his grandfather turn his back, nithyananda started researching every single book in the stall. Suddenly he jumped with great enthusiasm at a book that featured the great epic Ramayana with pictures for kids. The stall owner saw his enthusiasm for the book and asked him if he wanted to keep the book. By then, nithyananda had leafed through the book and replied, 'No! I don't want this book. I will look at some other book.' The owner asked why. nithyananda replied that the book was a misrepresentation of Ramayana and that instead of narrating the story with pictures for support, it appeared as though for the sake of pictures, they had made up the storyline.

The stall owner was shocked at the conviction, clarity and authority with which the boy was talking. He asked him, 'Why don't you narrate to me the Ramayana as you know it in its true form?' nithyananda jumped at the invitation and started narrating in earnest, from what he had heard from his grandfather and from what he had read in various books on Ramayana. The stories that his grandfather had told him became the substance of impromptu discourses, called '*kathakalakshepam*', in Tamil. The stall owner started understanding that the boy was no mere boy. He put him on the table, bowed to him and listened as tears streamed from his eyes.

nithyananda could not understand the emotions of the man but continued with the narration upon insistence from him. He finished after an hour and the group that had gathered around him by then clapped spontaneously.

The stall owner was by now overwhelmed. He touched the child's feet and repeated many times amidst sobs that the child was certainly bestowed with divine grace, else he would not be able to narrate the story with such ease and confidence at such a young age. nithyananda asked his grandfather what wrong he had done to make the man cry so much. His grandfather too was in a moved state. He explained to the young boy that he was crying with joy to hear such a small boy speak so eloquently.

Once they reached home, nithyananda got his grandfather's confirmation once more that he had not done any wrong to make the man cry and ran away with great relief to his dear altar!

An affair with the Elephant God

When nithyananda was about three, he was given an idol of Ganapati as a gift.

Ganapati or Ganesa or Vinayaka, as He is called otherwise, is the son of Lord Siva and Parvati. He is the most popular God with a potbelly and an elephant head and He rides on a mouse. Ganapati is always prayed to, before any practicing Hindu embarks on any serious venture, seeking His blessings for that venture. He is the remover of all obstacles and brings success. It is said that His own father Siva had to come back and pray to Him when He forgot to obtain His blessings before He went to battle a demon!

The legend of Ganapati, reads as follows.

Parvati was the daughter of Himavan, who was the King of the Himalayas. From birth, Parvati was in love with Siva, the Rejuvenator. She married Him against her father's wishes, since Himavan believed that Siva was a no good ascetic living off the land. He believed that Siva was not a good match for the daughter of a rich and powerful king.

One day as Parvati was bathing, Siva walked in unannounced. Parvati was upset at her husband's rude behavior and wanted some one to guard her privacy thereon. However, every one around her was under Siva's control and she wanted someone who would listen only to her.

Parvati removed the sandal wood paste that she had applied on her body and breathed life into it. A beautiful young child appeared before her. Parvati instructed this child to guard her privacy, irrespective of who the intruder was. As was His wont, Siva appeared on the scene one day and tried to barge in.

The child stopped Him. Angered and not wanting to fight with a child, Siva sent His hordes, the gana, to remove the child from the scene. The child made short work of Siva's gana and packed them off running.

Siva became furious and with His powerful trident cut the child's head off. Parvati came out of her bath and found her young child dead. Inconsolable and terrifying in her anger, she gave Siva an ultimatum: Revive the child or I go.

Siva sent what remained of His gana with the instruction to find the first body they could so that He could revive the child. What they found first was an elephant. Siva fixed the elephant's head on the child and he came alive.

Siva made this brave young boy the Master of His gana, giving the boy the name Ganesa or Ganapati.

There are hundreds of stories woven around this lovable child God who, along with Krishna, is the favorite of most Hindus.

nithyananda started worshipping the Ganapati idol with great devotion. The idol was not an inanimate statue to him; it was a living object. He related with the idol at a personal level. He would play for hours with the idol, bathe it, dress it, and feed it.

When nithyananda offered Ganapati food, he expected Ganapati to consume the food, and became upset when Ganapati did not eat the food offered to him. nithyananda would try cajoling Ganapati and try all the tricks he knew to persuade Ganapati to eat the food he offered Him. When in spite of all his cajoling Ganapati did not eat, nithyananda would threaten to drop the idol in the well that was in the center of the house.

Cajoling and threatening, he would give Ganapati a deadline to eat or else. He would wait for three to four hours even after giving Him this deadline. When Ganapati still did not oblige, nithyananda would place Him carefully along with some food, in a bucket, that was used to bring the water up from the well inside the house, and slowly lower Him by loosening the rope that was attached to the bucket.

At each level of lowering, nithyananda would cajole and threaten the idol again and again. He would harbor mixed emotions; anger that Ganapati did not listen to him, did not care for his threats; at another level, fear that if he did drop Him into the water, He might die.

When the bucket reached the bottom of the well and floated on top of the water, he would feel that he had carried out his threat far enough and that Ganapati by now would have eaten. He would bring Him up, to find to his chagrin that He had not eaten the food after all. Angered, nithyananda would lower the idol again, hoping that this time Ganapati would have better sense. When he brought Him up again the food would be untouched.

Lost in his anger, he would feel no longer any interest in threatening Ganapati; only compassion that Ganapati had not eaten!

Not knowing what to do and worried that his Ganapati would come to harm if he did not eat, nithyananda one day told his family members about it. They thought it was funny and laughed at him. They made fun of his childishness in trying to get the Ganapati idol to eat. They also worried that if nithyananda dropped the idol in the well, they would have to spend money in buying him another idol as replacement, and told him they would not buy him another one if he lost this idol.

Around this time, nithyananda heard the story of Nambiandar Nambi. Nambi's father was a priest in a temple. One day his father had to go on an errand, and told Nambi to carry out the daily *puja* ritual and also to offer food to God. Nambi took his father at his word and after the *puja*, placed some food in front of the idol, drew the cloth screen in front of the idol and waited for the idol to eat.

After a while when he looked in, the food was untouched. Nambi started crying. He felt he had made a grievous mistake and that God was angry with him and hence not eaten the food.

He was also afraid that his father, when he returned, would be angry with him for not doing the job entrusted to him properly. Nambi started bashing his head against the stonewall of the temple, telling the idol that if He did not eat the food offered to Him, he would break his own head and die. When he looked up after a few minutes, the food had been eaten.

When nithyananda heard this story, he was very upset and hurt. If God ate Nambi's food, why would He not eat nithyananda's food? Suddenly he realized that there was a difference: Nambi had tortured himself, hurt himself; he did not torture the idol; he did not threaten God like he himself did. Nambi did not lower his God into the well threatening to drown Him; instead he offered his own life.

nithyananda decided he would not eat if Ganapati did not eat. He placed some food in front of the idol and waited. When Ganapati did not eat, nithyananda did not eat his food as well. He would take the food from his mother, pretend he was going to eat, walk to the back of the house and dump it in the drain. This went on for two to three days. Each day Ganapati's food was replaced. nithyananda's parents were unaware of what was going on. Despite his hunger, the child kept his resolve and waited for Ganapati to eat, dumping his own food untouched.

At the end of the third day, the food in front of the idol disappeared! The child was overwhelmed with love and gratitude. Tears streamed down his cheeks. nithyananda's spiritual life started in earnest at this point in time. He had realized through personal experience, the power of devotion and faith. From then on, every day till the day of his own enlightenment, nithyananda would only eat after offering food to Ganapati. Only when He ate, nithyananda ate. After enlightenment, Nithyananda never ate; only He ate!

Ganesh Chaturthi: Awakening of Spiritual Inclinations

Right from early childhood, nithyananda was drawn to spirituality and as we saw earlier, he spent as much time as he could with idols; he interacted with them as if they were living beings, which to him they certainly were. He had a deep and abiding passion to play with idols of gods and goddesses, decorating them, worshipping them, talking to them, and relating to them as if they were made of flesh and blood. These were his only joy. He rarely participated in sports and games normal to boys of his age.

Parasakti (The universal or cosmic energy in the form of the universal Mother) indeed works in mysterious ways to help enlightened beings fulfill their mission.

During the period of *Ganesh Chaturthi,* the birthday of Lord Ganapati, potters would come to Tiruvannamalai town with large amounts of clay to make their idols of Ganapati. Each house would usually have an idol installed in their altar and people of that household would offer ritual prayers to the Ganapati idol. On the festival day, special food would be prepared to be offered to the Lord. Ganapati's favorite food is the *modakam* - a rice dumpling filled with unrefined brown sugar. In addition, there would be special fruits and flowers that Ganapati liked. After all, the fat bellied Ganapati sitting on his mouse vehicle is the darling of all Hindus!

Depending upon local tradition, on the third, fifth or tenth day after the festival day, the Ganapati idol would be taken and immersed in a water spot, an environmentally friendly practice, as long as the idol was made out of mud and is water soluble. In large cities, this immersion takes the form of massive processions to the sea. In smaller towns, the idols would be carried by individuals on their heads, or if they are wealthy, in vehicular transportation and then immersed in the temple tank or a near by lake.

Potters would bring in large quantities of clay for making the idols on the spot. They would leave behind unused material that they could not convert and sell. nithyananda would rush around on his tricycle, collecting all this material so that he could fashion his own idols out of this unused clay. Even at this early age his commercial sense was well developed.

The only person who would object to nithyananda bringing all the clay into the house was his maternal grandmother. He would throw some of the clay at her as well. The whole house would be filled with clay and half finished clay figures, a huge mess! nithyananda would also offer *puja* to all these clay idols, ringing his bell loudly from morning till evening intermittently. His grandmother would object to this as well strongly. nithyananda had learnt a *mantra* from a *Yogi* to drive ghosts and evil spirits away; he would use them as soon as his grandmother started fighting with him! It seemed to work, that and the constant bell ringing. This grandmother is still very much alive today, and in her nineties!

Nithyananda says:

'*Parasakti* (The universal Mother) prepared my body and mind so beautifully for the mission she had in mind for me. You can see her play, her *lila*. Day after day, I would spend entire days only in decorating and talking to the idols. I had energy and power far beyond my years. My mother said that once I turned around a heavy teak wood bed with a person lying on it without much effort!'

nithyananda was completely independent and fearless. His mother and the rest of the family used to listen to what he had to say, rather than the other way around. His sharp logic and compassionate love attracted people to him and made them want to do what he told them to.

Raghupati Yogi

When nithyananda was about three, he met Yogiraj Raghupati Maharaj, otherwise called Raghupati Yogi.

A relative brought home a mendicant, a *sanyasi.* It was common practice in his household to offer shelter and food to ascetics. nithyananda's grandfather used to feed at least ten such mendicants, every day at lunch. They would be seated in a row, fed, saluted with the traditional *arti* (obeisance with a lamp) and given money before they departed.

This *sanyasi,* named Raghupati Yogi, saw young nithyananda playing with idols and remarked that the boy was a light that had started shining in that household. nithyananda felt comfortable with this man and related to him his own experiences with Ganapati and how Ganapati ate the food that he served him after he threatened to go on a fast. Yogi seemed to understand him and was able to relate to what nithyananda was saying to him.

For as long as nithyananda could remember, whenever he was alone, he used to see a group of eleven people around himself. He got so used to seeing them that he used to think they were his relatives who were part of his joint family, till he realized that only he, and no one else could see them. When he met Raghupati Yogi and he had initiated him, these people stopped appearing. The boy asked Yogi about this. Raghupati Yogi told him that these people were *bhairava,* Siva *gana* or soldiers, who were protecting him till then. Now that he had been initiated and protected by the *Guru mantra,* they did not feel the need to be around him. He said, 'They have handed you over to me.'

nithyananda had names for each of these *bhairava*, and he used to recite their names faithfully before each meal. Years later, when he read the life of Sarada Devi, wife of Ramakrishna *Paramahamsa*, he learnt that just like the *bhairava* who surrounded him, Sarada Devi, as a child was surrounded by the *sakhi*, women companions of Devi, the Mother Goddess.

nithyananda maintained a diary where he used to write down all the stories that Raghupati Yogi had told him, as well as all incidents that happened during his interaction with him. Raghupati Yogi was meticulous in making the boy write down everything. When nithyananda left home, even though his family moved home a few times, his mother ensured that nithyananda's diaries were safely stored. Thanks to her, and to Raghupati Yogi, this information is available today for us.

Raghupati Yogi came into nithyananda's life for a purpose. He was perhaps not an enlightened Master, but certainly a *Yogi* of great skills and powers. He helped prepare nithyananda and his body to receive and hold the energy of enlightenment, which Nithyananda now says was like keeping four elephants in a small hut. Nithyananda remembers Raghupati Yogi with tremendous affection and respect.

Raghupati Yogi used to live on the same street as nithyananda and knew the entire family. He had been born and brought up in Burma, then a British Colony, and now Myanmar, where he had learnt *yogic* procedures from Buddhist lamas. He was an adept and could levitate. He would lift himself up and ask children to move under him to check that there was nothing supporting him, to prove that what he was doing was no magic or illusion. He would do this through a combination of *yogic* postures, *asana*, and breath control, *pranayama*.

Sometimes, he would exhale completely emptying his lungs out, and fasten tightly around his chest an iron clamp. He would then inhale and inflate his chest, breaking the iron clamp into pieces! He would capture snakes, put them into his nose and have them come out through his mouth!

Many scientific experiments have been conducted, notably by Harvard University's Medical College, through Dr. Howard Johnson and others, on extraordinary *yogic* powers that Tibetan Lamas have acquired though controlled breathing and meditation. These include increasing body temperature, levitation and many extraordinary physical feats of strength not normally possible by humans.

Raghupati Yogi used to eat very little, if at all. He had special techniques to control hunger and thirst that he later taught nithyananda. When his disciples forced him to eat out of concern, he would eat a little and then snap his fingers. His intestines would come out through his mouth. He would clean his intestines of all food matter and put it back. He was an expert on Patanjali's *ashtanga yoga* methods and used these techniques to prepare nithyananda's body and mind.

Raghupati Yogi would without fail come to nithyananda's house in the morning every day. He started calling him '*samiar*', the respectful Tamil word for an ascetic or Master, and this name was then used by everyone including nithyananda's parents to refer to him. Yogi would take him to the temple and for three to four hours each day make him practice Yoga techniques. Over time, he taught all eight parts of the *ashtanga yoga*, including *pranayama* and *asana*. After the Yoga practice, he would take the boy to breakfast. He was very loving and brought the boy candies and chocolates to keep the boy's interest alive.

nithyananda related with him easily and asked him many questions that he would answer patiently. When elderly people he knew came to talk to Yogi when he was with nithyananda, he would tell them, 'Don't think I am teaching this boy, I'm learning from him.'

One day Raghupati Yogi asked nithyananda whether he wished to visit Kailash, the abode of Lord Siva and Parvati, nithyananda at once said 'yes,' he would. He told him that he would initiate nithyananda into a *mantra*, which if he repeated, would take him to see Siva and Parvati in Kailash. Yogi asked nithyananda to return the next day and meet him at the temple.

When nithyananda met Yogi the next day in the *Kartika mandapam* in the temple, the first thing he wanted to know was where the bus that would take them to Kailash was! Yogi laughed and pointed to one of the tourist buses parked in front of the temple and told the young boy that one of those buses would take them to Kailash. He then asked nithyananda to bathe in the temple tank and come to him. nithyananda came after bathing in the tank and sat in front of him, on a step below where Yogi sat. Yogi uttered the word *'hreem'*. Something seemed to strike nithyananda at his '*hara*', the point between the *Swadishthana* and *Muladhara* energy centers, between his navel and the bottom of his spine. nithyananda saw Devi, Goddess Parvati standing in front of him. He laughed in ecstasy, and shouted, '*amma* (mother) is here, *amma* is here!'

nithyananda had no idea that '*hreem*' was the *bija mantra* (invocation sound) of Devi or that She would appear before him. He was hoping to catch a bus to Kailash! The vision of Devi was clear and vivid. After a few moments, Devi merged into the young boy. 'I saw Her' he said to Yogi, in wonder, 'I saw Her with four hands!'

Raghupati Yogi did not believe the boy at first. He thought that it was nithyananda's active imagination. The boy was filled with ecstasy. When nithyananda went home, he picked up a nail and flattened it into a chisel of sorts. He then picked up a soft stone and carved the figure and form of Devi as he saw her. After many attempts, still not satisfied, he took the idol to a stone Carver, who he was acquainted with and requested him to finish it. (This sandstone Devi idol is displayed today at the ashram for everyone to see.)

Nithyananda took the finished carving to Raghupati Yogi. 'This is the *Amma* that I saw when you gave me the *mantra,*' he told him. Raghupati Yogi asked nithyananda to sit and held his hands. Normally the boy would feel energy flowing into him from the *Yogi*; this time around he felt that energy was flowing from him to the *Yogi*!

Yogi stood up and prostrated himself at the boy's feet. nithyananda cried out, 'what are you doing, *thatha*?' *Thatha* meaning grandfather in Tamil. Yogi said, 'All these years I had the *mantra* and used it, but I had no experience. I was like a librarian with all the books, without knowing and experiencing the content. I planted the seed and waited. Now, the seed has sprouted!'

He added, 'I am blessed, my child. It takes years to see Devi. You are indeed a *Siddha Purusha* (a realized being). That's why you could have Her vision just after initiation. Devi is hereafter your *ishta devata*, your favorite deity!'

Raghupati Yogi would take nithyananda to a local vegetarian restaurant for breakfast. One day the owner of the restaurant where they used to eat, Ramachandra Upadhyaya, came up to Yogi and complained that he did not have enough *sanyasis* to feed that day. This man had the practice of feeding fifty *sanyasis* on every *Amavasya* (new moon day), and he did not have that many to feed on that *Amavasya* day. The *yogi* said to him, 'You are feeding this young boy, that's enough; it is equivalent to feeding a 1000 *sanyasis*!'

It is a different matter that neither nithyananda nor Upadhyaya believed the *yogi*. Recently, Upadhyaya performed *pada puja* (ritual obeisance to the Master's feet) to Nithyananda and recalled that incident. He said to Nithyananda, 'I was so blessed to feed tens of thousands of holy men by just feeding you as a boy.'

One day, nithyananda asked Raghupati Yogi why he was teaching him all these *yoga asana,* since the *yogi* himself did not achieve Devi's *darshan* through these practices. The yogi said that nithyananda needed to keep his body fit, as he would need to do Herculean things in future.

Day after day, Raghupati Yogi would make the boy do these *yogic* exercises. He would make him climb the stone pillars in the temple. The boy had to climb at least 24 pillars each day. The boy obeyed him, partly out of respect and partly out of affection. Moreover, he didn't have to suffer at school! If nithyananda had homework and complained to the Yogi, the teacher would fall sick the next day!

Yogi told nithyananda that the age to learn yoga is before 14, and that's why he started him at 3 so that he had 10 full years to train him. He taught him *asanas*, *pranayama*, *dhyana*, *mantra* and various other techniques. Yogi could do magical things with sounds. With one sound he could attract dogs from hundreds of yards away. He could break a stone by making the sound of a hammer hitting on stone. With another sound he could make people invisible. When the school watchman came looking for nithyananda when he did not go to school, the boy would run to the *Yogi*. The *Yogi* would make a sound and even though the boy would be standing right in front of both the watchman and the *Yogi*, the watchman would not be able to see him.

Nithyananda says:

'After the age of 14, only an enlightened Master can be in true *Brahmacharya,* which is one of the five *yama,* forming part of *ashtanga yoga*.

With no disrespect to the tradition of *sanyasins*, let me put on record that they cannot be in *Brahmacharya* unless they become enlightened. I say this to my ashramites, to the young *Brahmacharis* in the ashram: Do not feel guilty for lapses. You are staying unmarried only to avoid marital problems! Being single for you is not a spiritual vow, but a social vow.' That was the reason why Raghupati Yogi started training me at such an early age so that before adolescence I could master these practices, and be spiritually prepared.'

Raghupati Yogi did a great service by preparing nithyananda's body and mind for his future endeavors. He also had his own fulfillment. As much as nithyananda learnt from him, the *yogi* said he learnt from the boy. He gave nithyananda deerskin he used to sit on, which was given to him by his Master. This was treated and tanned with herbs, and even after 60 odd years has the original hair on it. The skin is now at the ashram in Bangalore, India.

Raghupati Yogi taught nithyananda how to go without water, without feeling thirsty, by twisting the tongue, sucking in air, while sounding the *mantra* 'lam'. He gave the boy a herb with which by drawing a diagram in one's liver area one could go without food, without feeling any hunger. He taught the boy how to go without sleep, without feeling tired. He taught him how to play with life energy and how to create things through sound energy. These were of immense use to nithyananda during his wandering days and penance; but for these techniques and the strength built in through yoga, his mind body would not have been able to withstand the rigors of those years of tough ascetic life.

Raghupati Yogi could materialize objects. He could control snakes. Though an accomplished *yogi,* he was not enlightened. Upon insistence from young nithyananda to demonstrate the miraculous powers that yoga could bestow, the levitating yogi materialized a conch for him. nithyananda was astonished and examined the conch to find a date inscribed on it. He accused the *yogi* of cheating him! The *yogi* explained to him that he had not created it for him; he had merely teleported it from his home, miles away. He also explained to the child that these feats were not a measure of spirituality or Self Realization and that they were mere play with energy.

When nithyananda was barely ten, Raghupati Yogi arranged a public function in which nithyananda spoke on Patanjali's *Yoga Sutra*! He told him that he was ready to give discourses in public and that the program was like an initiation from him to the boy to become an *acharya*, a teacher. Yogi distributed flyers announcing nithyananda as his disciple. Over a thousand people attended this discourse by the young lad. Nithyananda remembers that this event was video recorded. The venue was in front of the *Raja Gopuram* (main temple tower) in Tiruvannamalai where the popular *Irai Mani Mandram* every year is held.

Raghupati Yogi arranged for taking pictures of nithyananda in various meditative postures during his years with him. Photography was very expensive in those days in rural India. Yogi had borrowed money from the hotel owner Upadhyaya for taking these photographs. When asked why he was doing it at such expense, he simply smiled, never answered. When the photos were delivered, he wrote on them, 'The whole world will thank me one day for these photographs!'

It is these pictures that we see today of young nithyananda in meditation; at the age of about 9, his first photographs. Raghupati Yogi had photographs made of both nithyananda and himself together, but none of himself alone. The boy questioned him about this as well, 'why don't you have a photo of yourself so that I can keep it?' Raghupati Yogi just smiled and said, 'No one will want to worship my photographs; but they will worship yours!'

The photographer who took these pictures recollects that when he was taking the pictures of both Raghupati Yogi and Nithyananda in meditation, both of them levitated, rising above the ground a clear few inches.

Deep insights into Yoga from the Consciousness of Patanjali

Nithyananda recounted to us recently in Los Angeles, USA about his days with Raghupati Yogi:

I had the great fortune to be around this great Master called Raghupathi Yogi. When I met him, he was around 105 years of age!
He was from the lineage of Patanjali. Patanjali is the founder of the

Yoga system. He is the first Master who created a clear scientific and logical system to reproduce the experience of enlightenment. Until Patanjali, enlightenment was an accident; somebody may get it or not get it. It was more like gambling. You had to play, but there was no guarantee. Patanjali was the first Master, I can say spiritual navigator, who actually did the mapping and gave the complete directions. He created clear cut directions; step by step formulae to reproduce the experience of enlightenment!

Like how scientists create a formula to reproduce the understanding of the outer world things, Patanjali created a beautiful formula, a technology to reproduce the inner world experience, enlightenment itself. And Ragupathi Yogi had mastered the whole Science. Not only the physical aspect of yoga like bending the body etc., what we call asana, or hatha yoga, but also the other aspects of yoga like working with your breath - prana, working with the mind, working with the visualization power, emotions etc. He had mastered all other dimensions of yoga as well.

Between the ages of 3 and 13, when I was with him, he prepared my body, he prepared the mind to enter into the experience of enlightenment and to stay in the experience of enlightenment. Entering also is not a big thing; to have a glimpse of satori – the no-mind state, to have one experience of un-clutching from the mind is not a big thing; it's not very difficult, but to stay in that, not only to stay in that, but to express that energy through your body, for that, your body and mind need to be prepared. That is the real thing! Just having one glimpse is not a big thing; anybody can have it. But staying in that same space, staying in that same Consciousness and expressing it, needs preparation. He focused on that part and helped me in so many ways to understand and experience, and above all, to stay in that same space; to stay in that high energy plane and radiate that experience.

From morning six or seven o'clock, he would start the training. At that time, it was practically a torture! He would make me bend in all possible ways. In the Arunachala temple where he used to teach me yoga, there was this beautiful stone pillar hall. He would make me climb all the stone pillars! 20 to 30 pillars I had to climb one after the other. Till date, I am not able to find any reference any yoga book as to why one should climb pillars to do yoga! (laughter). And he will make me climb with only one hand for support. I had to use only one hand and climb the pillar and come down.

He also used to give me practice in Neti, one dimension of yoga where he would make me swallow a long cloth to clean the intestine and the system. I tell you honestly: only now I feel happy about all these things. In those days I used to hate him!

Some of the insights he gave on Patanjali's words were revealing and shocking and sometimes even contradicting. He explained that the words of Patanjali were captured in the books, but not his body language. So naturally, much is lost. Only a person who has experienced the Consciousness of Patanjali can bring Patanjali back to life. And I had the great fortune to be with the Master who has experienced that Consciousness, or the same inner space of Patanjali, because of which he was able to reveal the deeper truths of the Science of Yoga.

I asked him why he made me climb those pillars because I did not find any reference to climbing pillars in any yoga book. He gave me a beautiful explanation: For any purpose that you bend your body, move your body, that purpose, that memory with which you are doing it, that idea, will get completely inserted or recorded into your body and mind. This is a very shocking revelation. He says: with any intention if you move your body, bend your body, or make your body active, that intention, that purpose will be recorded into your body; that purpose, that idea, that samskara will start expressing in your body.

He means: the way in which you bend, the method in which you stand up, or the method in which you do yoga are not really important. The intention, if you have an intention to have health, and do whatever you want for that intention, if you move your body in a particular way for that intention, health will simply happen to you.

He says even ordinary sitting, if you strongly believe that by sitting you will have health, you will see that health happens in you when you sit with that intention. I asked him how it was possible and he laughed and replied that the body itself is made out of our memory. We are an expression of our own self hypnosis. Every type of memory is recorded in our muscles. So when we change the memories, we can change our system also.

Nithyananda says that Raghupati Yogi was an incarnation of Patanjali.

Patanjali in turn was an incarnation of the great snake Adisesha, upon whom Vishnu rests. Once when Siva danced in Kailash, one of his anklets burst open, and to avoid Siva stopping his dance, Adisesha wrapped himself upon Siva's ankle as an anklet. When Siva finished His dance, He blessed the snake, who said to him, 'All others enjoyed your dance, but being on your ankle I could not. Please give me the opportunity to see you dance.'

Siva said, 'You will be born on Earth and after penance you shall see Me dance.'

Accordingly, Adisesha was born as Patanjali in Chidambaram, and Siva came and danced for him as Nataraja.

When Nithyananda told us this incident, many of us recollected the number of times His own anklets have broken loose during his dances at the time of *Ananda Darshan*; heavy anklets of gold giving way with the energy of His dance.

Yogi Ram Surat Kumar - Visiri Swamigal

nithyananda befriended a number of other sages as well in early childhood. One of them, Saakkupai Swami, wore only jute cloth from gunny bags (called *saakkupai* in Tamil) and slept in the temple. Children were scared of him and avoided him. nithyananda went to Saakkupai Swami and asked how he could see Arunachala in human form. Saakkupai Swami laughed and said, 'Don't cheat me, go away, go away'. nithyananda ran away frightened. When he turned around to see what the Swami was doing, nithyananda was surprised to see him prostrating on the ground in his direction.

After that incident, whenever nithyananda passed his way, Saakkupai Swami would throw candies and sweets towards him though the boy would not go near him. nithyananda thought that this man was mad. One day, nithyananda threw a rupee coin at Saakkupai Swami. Saakkupai Swami said he did not need money; nithyananda asked whether he could bring him food. Saakkupai Swami said, 'No, instead bring me *beedis'* (local cigarettes made of cured tobacco leaves). nithyananda bought a packet of *beedis* and gave it to him, which Saakkupai Swami kept by his side. Soon a dog came and picked up the *beedis* and ran away. Saakkupai Swami told nithyananda to follow the dog. The dog ran and reached Yogi Ram Surat Kumar, popularly known as Visiri Swamigal, and placed the packet in front of him. Visiri Swamigal started smoking the *beedis.*

Visiri Swamigal sat amidst a pile of garbage that he had collected on the steps of the building adjacent to Thermutti, where the temple chariot was parked. He was an enlightened Master, well-known and well-liked in Tiruvannamalai. He was a contemporary of Bhagwan Sri Ramana Maharishi. Visiri Swamigal turned to nithyananda and asked him whether Saakkupai Swamigal had sent him to him. nithyananda explained to him how he got there and how he had gotten to know Saakkupai Swamigal. Visiri Swamigal took a liking to the young boy and they became instant friends.

After a few days, Visiri Swamigal offered a *beedi* to nithyananda. Having been taught that smoking was a bad habit, nithyananda refused. Who knows, his enlightenment may have been faster had he accepted the Mystic's offer of a *beedi*!

It was customary for people who passed Visiri Swamigal, to stop by and ask him questions about their future. Children on their way to school would stop by and ask how they would fare in their exams. They could rarely elicit a response from the intriguing Mystic. One day, nithyananda on his way to school, stopped by and asked if he would pass in his test in school that day. He got a reply, 'You will pass the test of life, my boy!' nithyananda could not comprehend the meaning of those words. A lady who sat hearing this told him, 'Go on child! You will not understand these words now; but you will recall them later!'

Some of the famous graveyards of the holy town of Tiruvannamalai were serene places of meditation for nithyananda. A couple of years back, as we walked as a small group with the Master in the wee hours of the morning in Tiruvannamalai, he took us to these graveyards and showed us the exact spots where he would sit and meditate. He also pointed out to a large tomb and said, 'Do you see that large tomb there? That double bed there! That is where Yogi Ram Surat Kumar used to be sitting. I used to hide and watch him and enjoy the mysticism that he radiated. He would shoo me away saying: its only me, go away!'

He recalled that one-day, when he was returning home from his graveyard meditation, he saw a man lying across the pathway prostrating in the direction of Arunachala, which was a customary practice in Tiruvannamalai. He waited for him to get up so he could go through. The man never got up and nithyananda suddenly realized that it was a dead body! Unmoved, he jumped over and went on his way. His increasing spiritual zeal held no place for fear, sorrow or any other emotion that might have stalled his race towards merging with the Divine.

Mystique of Arunachala

From childhood, nithyananda's grandfather used to tell him mythological stories and nithyananda used to repeat them with great flourish to other family members. They were all amused at the young boy's great interest in spiritual matters and imitating Raghupati Yogi started calling him *samiar,* or *swami,* which in Tamil referred to an ascetic or monk. Even his parents started calling him *swami.*

nithyananda was in love with Arunachala. He joined every temple procession and followed it all the way till it ended. He spent his days in the temple and ate with the *sanyasis,* who were given free food at the temple. The temple of Arunachaleshwara in Tiruvannamalai was nithyananda's playfield, as Brindavan was to Krishna and Dakshineshwar was to Ramakrishna.

When he woke up in the morning in his house, nithyananda would walk with closed eyes to the front of the house, so that the Arunachala hill was the first thing that he saw in the morning. His brothers and sister used to call him *kuruttu samiar* or blind monk! They used to irritate him by standing in front of him as he opened his eyes, or by turning him around so that he faced the opposite direction, or by startling him by shouting at him. nithyananda used to kick them, rave and rant, and go back to bed and start all over again.

To nithyananda, Arunachala, the hill, was a living entity, not a mere formation of rocks. He would sit contemplating the hill, like in Zen meditation, *Zazen*; sitting, happening, without knowing.

Telepathic Old Man and the Silent Sage

When he was about seven, nithyananda met Narayanaswami Thatha known as K.S. Narayanaswami (*thatha* means grandfather in Tamil). Thatha lived in a small Ganapati temple on Thirumanjana Gopuram Street in Tiruvannamalai. He was a master of *tantra*, *yantra* and *mantra*, all the three techniques of realization. He had great powers of telepathy. The local police would come to him seeking help in identifying perpetrators of crime.

Thatha would take a mirror and draw a square on it; the picture of the criminal would appear within that square. People who lost things and people who lost children and relatives would come to him and he would show them where they were on his mirror. nithyananda watched him do this untiringly day after day.

nithyananda spent six years around Narayanaswamy Thatha. When people came seeking his help, Thatha would light a lamp, and mutter some *mantra.* He would then collect the black soot from the lamp and apply it on the mirror that he had. Immediately, the picture of what had happened would be played out as if on television. The entire sequence of what happened, whether it was a burglary or a person missing, would be played out. The local Police Inspector would come and sit at Thatha's feet.

Thieves used to come to him begging not to be disclosed to the Police. When he gave them his assurance, the mirror would not show anything. He would make them give away their money or part of their money to the temple; sometimes make them return their money if they had looted a good man. Each day he accumulated thousands of rupees.

Whatever Thatha earned, whatever people gave him for his services, he would give away the same day, since he had taken a vow not to accumulate any material property or money. Ascetics and beggars would crowd around him to take what he gave away. nithyananda used to bring him food from home, as his mother was quite generous in feeding spiritual people. nithyananda was his errand boy, happy watching the television show in the mirror, getting to know all the gossip in town, and sharing the joy of those who found what they came seeking.

Once, the idol from a temple in a nearby village Tiruneer Annamalai was stolen by breaking the idol from the foundation. Thatha's mirror showed that the idol was buried in a disused water tank, and the Police found it. Since the original temple was broken into and the foundation was damaged, Thatha asked the Police to build a temple within the Police Station, and they did! Thatha's mirror too is in this temple. This probably is the only temple built inside a Police Station in India, or perhaps anywhere else in the world!

One day, when Thatha was in the bathroom, nithyananda decided to inspect the mirror. He applied the black ash to the mirror, but he had nothing to ask. Suddenly, the form of Devi appeared in the mirror. She smiled at him. nithyananda was afraid she would tell Thatha that he used the mirror. He sat down and prayed to her, 'Please do not tell him.' She seemed to smile saying she would not tell him. But the problem was how to make her go away.

When Thatha came out of the bathroom, nithyananda showed him the mirror and confessed. He just laughed. He said, 'If Devi did not wish to appear, She would not have. You didn't do anything wrong.' Thatha gave nithyananda the silver box in which he used to keep the mirror. This box is in the ashram in Bangalore today.

Often when nithyananda missed school, he would seek the help of Thatha to escape punishment from teachers. Thatha would make sure nithyananda's attendance in school was marked.

Thatha used to materialize objects. He also would provide people solutions to their problems. Once, a low caste man came to Thatha with a problem and Thatha advised him to go around a Siva temple three times. The man said that in his village he would not be allowed into the temple being a low caste person. Thatha then pointed to nithyananda and told the man to go around him three times. When he did so, Thatha told the man that his problems were solved. Neither the man nor nithyananda understood the meaning of what had happened; but the man's problem did get resolved.

From Narayanaswami Thatha, nithyananda learnt the science of *tantra, mantra* and *yantra*, and how they worked, and how they should be used. *Tantra* are the meditation techniques used to attain enlightenment; *mantra* is any repetitive holy chant that is also a path to enlightenment; *yantra* is a metaphorical representation of the cosmos on a copper plate, which is used as a meditative tool for attaining enlightenment. Once nithyananda asked Thatha to provide him with a *mantra* to which Thatha replied that there was no need for that, since nithyananda had his own *mantra,* a thousand times more powerful; but over time he taught him many techniques including *mantra.*

Once, after installing the Devi idol in the Police Station temple, Thatha called nithyananda to him saying, '*Chinnapaiya* (little boy), come and learn from me'.

nithyananda said, 'I have learnt a lot from you. You taught me many things, *mantras* and techniques. What else do you want me to learn?'

Thatha said, 'If your mind is pure; it does not need *mantra* to effect any miracles. In your presence alone, miracles will happen.'

It was as if a chord deep inside nithyananda was struck by these words. He said to Narayanaswami Thatha, 'Then you should have purified my mind instead of teaching me all those *mantras*, which you say are of no use.

In response, Thatha said, 'Don't worry; these *mantras* will purify your mind.'

From that day, nithyananda stopped the practice of *mantra* and *tantra* that he had been taught.

Narayanaswamy Thatha gave nithyananda a *yantra* and a book of chants. He also instructed him on the *mooligai prana prathishta mantra* which when chanted to herbal plants a thousand times facing East, would impart permanence to them so that even when plucked or cut they will retain their natural powers.

Whenever nithyananda took leave of Thatha at the end of each day, he would bless the boy silently and hand over a fruit from his collection. One day, when the boy took leave with the traditional Tamil '*poyuttu varen*' (shall go and return), Thatha uncharacteristically said 'Go' and instead of handing him a fruit indicated that he pick one from the plate himself. The third day after this incident, Thatha passed away. His *samadhi*, the place of burial still exists in Tiruvannamalai, in the name of *Thottakara Thatha* or Gardener Grandfather, the name by which he was popularly known.

nithyananda as was his wont, continued to develop more spiritual connections. He met a *sanyasi* who used to sit in the Arunachala temple near the Thirumanjana Gopuram. This *sanyasi*, Narayana Swamigal was quite popular in Tiruvannamalai. He was called *Mouna Swamigal* or Silent Sage, as he never used to speak. He never used to eat as well. Whenever someone went to him to seek blessings, he would raise both his hands and stand in that posture for ten minutes. He had a small slate board on which was written in Tamil '*summa iru sollaren*' which meant 'just be silent'. He sat truly silently, without inner chatter. Whenever nithyananda sat with Mouna Swamigal, he too felt the peace of inner silence. Mouna Swamigal is still alive. He has moved up the Arunachala hill, to a lonely spot where he has been living without food or water for 15 years.

Right from childhood, nithyananda's energy attracted people of similar energy and attitude, who willingly helped the child move forward in his chosen spiritual path. nithyananda's encounters with sages and ascetics right from early childhood kindled in the child a deep desire to emulate them.

The Math Master

The divinity in young nithyananda never missed the eye of the ardent seeker.

During his school days, one day, he was late to the math class. He stood in the doorway waiting for permission to enter. The math teacher was bent over his table. As nithyananda stood at the doorway, as if prompted by some intuition, the teacher looked up in his direction. He appeared to be in a trance at what he saw. He slowly raised and joined both his palms and saluted the boy with deep reverence. nithyananda was indeed intrigued!

The math teacher later urged nithyananda to visit him with his parents. Duly, nithyananda went to his house with his parents. At his house, as soon as he saw the boy, the math master prostrated at his feet and disclosed with great joy and emotion, that he had seen his favorite deity – Lord Ayyapa – in the boy, when he had stood in the doorway of the math class. He declared himself the boy's disciple. nithyananda was at a loss for words.

Isolated incidents of interest

An incident that Nithyananda delights in recounting of his early days of childhood is as follows:

In small towns such as Tiruvannamalai, during festival days, local groups with declared thespian talent would come forth to put up performances. Given the societal considerations still prevalent, in almost all these performances, men would act the role of women as well.
These shows would be attended mainly by children and old women who had not much work to do. Old women would sit around chewing tobacco and spitting the juice out. They would cover what they spat out with small mounds of earth. At the end of the show there would be many such mounds all over the place where these women sat.

One of the more popular shows was on the epic Mahabharata, the story of the rift between two ruling clans that ends in a great war, at the end of which Lord Krishna delivered the timeless truth of the Bhagavad Gita. In the Mahabharata, one of the most powerful and moving scenes is that of Princess Draupadi, the common wife of the five Pandava Princes, being disrobed in the royal court of the Kauravas, the mortal enemies and cousins of the Pandavas.

Dushassana, the Kaurava Prince is the arch villain in this drama. He insults Draupadi and attempts to outrage her modesty. Draupadi's husbands, the Pandava Princes are helpless as they are bound by codes of honor not to interfere.

Draupadi has no one to turn to except Lord Krishna. She throws up her hands and pleads in helplessness and surrender to Krishna, and lo, wonder of wonders, as each piece of clothing is removed a new set of clothes appear endlessly. Tired, bewildered and frightened Dushassana gives up, and Draupadi's honor is saved.

In the drama that nithyananda watched, Draupadi's role was performed by a man. This man normally wore seven saris and the cue was that when the sixth sari was removed by Dushassana Draupadi would call out to Krishna who would then jump on to the stage and save Draupadi's honor.

On that fateful day, Draupadi while dressing wore only six saris instead of seven, blissfully oblivious of the fact. On stage, he suddenly realized his mistake and started screaming aloud for Dushassana to let go of him. Even as Draupadi protested, Dushassana was intent upon removing the sixth and last sari as well. Draupadi kicked and screamed but Dushassana was playing his role in a dutiful fashion, keeping a correct count of the number of saris. Meanwhile the actor playing Krishna was smoking a local cigarette outside, oblivious of the trauma his dear Draupadi was going through!

Finally Dushassana succeeded. Draupadi stood on stage, a man clad only in boxer shorts and a blouse worn by women on top. Draupadi then screamed out, 'Oh Krishna! I called you so many times, and I almost gave up. This evil Dushassana disrobed and tried to shame me in public. But I am so grateful to you. To save my honor you transformed me into a man!'

The Master shakes with laughter as he narrates this story. It is a treat to watch him relating these stories, and to watch his expression as he goes back to his childhood days and relives the memories, not missing a single detail.

Once in a while he talks about the only movie that he watched, with his father and mother. It was a Tamil movie called 'Mudal Mariyadai' playing at the Balasubramanian theatre in Tiruvannamalai. Halfway through the movie he says he was frightened by some of the scenes where a person bites off some one's toe and swallows it. He walked away from the movie hall. He never again saw a movie or watched the television in childhood. nithyananda had never known fear before. Now he felt that fear was trying to get into him. He became conscious of this happening and so left the theatre.

When we watch television or a movie, the frames per second played through them are so high that they directly penetrate our consciousness. Watching a horror movie or a depressing movie for more than 20 minutes will infuse that mood into us; repetitive watching of such movies will shape our character without our knowing. That's why it is dangerous, especially for children who are very vulnerable in being influenced, to be allowed to watch violent or horror films. Even for adults, we should make it a practice not to watch for more than 15 minutes at a stretch any negatively emotional content on television or theatre.

As nithyananda grew up, his wild energy sometimes manifested itself in fits of actions. Once on a family trip to Tirupati with aunts, uncles, cousins and other relatives, he shared a room with some of his male relatives. As per his customary routine, he woke up at 3 am to perform his daily *puja*. While he was absorbed in his *puja*, an irate relative mumbled in his sleep about the disturbance caused. nithyananda walked up calmly to the man, caught him by his throat and is believed to have threatened to finish him off if he proved a hindrance to his *puja,* after which he serenely walked back and resumed his worship! Dissenting relatives stopped voicing open comments about the boy's activities thereafter!

As days rolled by, nithyananda's wild energy got canalized into his fierce spiritual quest. One day, he was with a cousin of his who had had enough of his mischievous and zealous antics. After a particularly trying encounter, the cousin flung a heavy object at him causing a deep gash on his forehead with heavy bleeding. After this incident, nithyananda is said to have visibly sobered down to the surprise and relief of all who knew him. Years later, nithyananda came to learn that through an accidental fall, Vivekananda carried a similar wound from childhood on his eyebrow as he did after the incident. Ramakrishna *Paramahamsa*, Vivekananda's Guru is said to have clarified that had the wound not occurred, the enormous energy that young Vivekananda was carrying would have been too strong for his physical body to sustain. Strange indeed are the ways of Existence!

Sage and a Child

The child in Nithyananda is waiting to be released at every opportunity. Time and again, in totally unpredictable manner as far as the rest of us are concerned, He would take us by surprise in His expressions of child like spontaneity.

Once, while in the process of discussing something quite serious, I unpacked some gifts from a devotee, which contained battery-operated toys. Instructions given to me were to fit the batteries and hand them over to Him. As He saw me fiddling with the batteries, He snatched the batteries and toys from me, saying, 'the fun is in fitting the batteries!'

The rest of the serious discussion was punctuated by His switching the toys on and off, making infernal noise.

While handing over the toys to Him I said, 'Perhaps these were sent for Anandi', referring to an eight year old disciple, the youngest member of the ashram. He pouted and responded, 'Were you told that? These are for Me!'

Of course, at the end of a few hours of play, the toys did go to Anandi!

Watching Him at these moments have been the greatest learning experiences for us. If an enlightened Master could behave like a child, absolutely unconcerned about what anyone may think of his action, totally in spontaneity, what reason for the rest of us to carry our petty fears of what others might say?

In many ways, His behavior is still very much like what we learn of His childhood experiences, curious, simple and spontaneous.

Previous Births

Many people have asked Nithyananda whether He is the reincarnation of one Master or another. At one level, His explanation is that all enlightened beings merge back again into universal energy and therefore energies of all enlightened Masters are the same.

Yet, at another level, there seem to be traits that are carried forward. Krishna, when He reappears, may not carry the flute and wear peacock feathers, but may still be the *Poornavatar* in subsequent reincarnations.

Nithyananda has indicated at various points in time that His last incarnation was about 300 years ago in the South of India. He says that at the appropriate time this information will be made available. Till then, we just enjoy His presence!

Chapter - 5

Siva Appears in human form

God as a friend

Nithyananda says:

'Enlightenment is not an end by itself. It is just the beginning of a spiritual journey. It is the threshold of a longer path, not a destination'.

We have talked about incarnations in earlier pages. Enlightened spirits, who do not need to be reborn as a result of their accumulated *samskara*, still reincarnate in planet Earth. They do not need to be born again, unlike ordinary mortals, since they have dissolved all their *vasana, samskara, and karma.* As we read earlier, our carried over desires and mental attitudes, based on our past actions, cause rebirth and the cycle of life and death. Once this *karmic* load is extinguished, and enlightenment results, this cycle stops. An enlightened being has no automatic rebirth.

It is true that in locations in this Universe of ours, other than planet Earth, living beings with intelligence, such as human beings, exist. However, it is only from planet Earth, can a conscious being proceed towards enlightenment, which is the state of super consciousness. Enlightened beings come back to planet Earth as incarnations, based on a need expressed by Mother Earth. They are recalled, as it were, and sucked back as energy by a desperate need upon this planet for their presence. The spiritual positivism of enlightened beings is needed to counteract the accumulated negativity of the planet.

It is in this context that Krishna announced in the Bhagavad Gita: Age after age, I shall be reborn upon this planet Earth, to protect the good and to eliminate the evil.

Enlightened beings have no free will, none at all. On the contrary, we, ordinary mortals, *do* have free will and use it. This is an irony of sorts. Human beings can actually choose to do what they want, and accumulate burdens of *samskara* and *karma* based on actions arising out of their free will. It is nature's way of making us responsible for our actions. Once we evolve spiritually, we understand more about the joy and freedom of surrendering our free will to the universe. By giving up the free will, which we understand in our limited way as freedom, we acquire true freedom, liberation. Surrendering one's freewill to the divine is the last step in the process of one's enlightenment.

This surrender of freewill is complete in an enlightened being. It is surrender and intellectual acceptance of all that is true; that divinity is resident within; that one's true nature is divine. In addition, it is the emotional acceptance of the divine within oneself; not just the intellectual understanding from the head, as it were, but the heartfelt emotional identification with that divinity within as well. Finally, it is a surrender of the senses; a complete acceptance through one's sensory perceptions to see reality as it is, not the way one's mind would want to interpret this reality. At this stage, one would be able to perceive the formless beyond the seen form, and accept the formless as divine. One would at this stage move and flow with the universe as the universe intends, with no intention of freewill.

Enlightened beings have already surrendered to the universe; intellectually, emotionally and through their senses. They have no longer the freedom to do what they wish. Whatever they do is directed by the universe, the divine. Enlightened beings are fully aware of their own inner divinity and this awareness in the form of divinity drives every one of their actions. Their mission in life is dictated by the universal intelligence.

Master says to us often:

'To all of you, 'God' is just a concept; and 'I' is reality. To me, 'God' is reality; God is a real experience and 'I' a mere concept; it is not real.'

The very first awareness of His own inner nature, His very first brush with His incarnated being, and the first revelation of His life's mission, happened to nithyananda when he met with Arunagiri Yogiswara, when he was about nine years of age.

Within the temple of Arunachala in Tiruvannamalai, at the rear of the main building housing the shrine of the deity Arunachaleshwara, is the *jiva samadhi*, the burial place or crypt, of Arunagiri Yogiswara.

Arunagiri Yogiswara is considered to be an incarnation of Lord Siva Himself. Without knowing why, as a child, nithyananda was attracted to the location of Arunagiri Yogiswara's *jiva samadhi* as he grew up and started spending a lot of his time there inside the Arunachala temple. nithyananda took to sitting in front of the *jiva samadhi* of Arunagiri Yogiswara.

One day, as nithyananda was sitting on this spot, he saw a handsome young man emerge from a dark corner of this *jiva samadhi*. This young man came up to him and started talking to him. nithyananda found him to be quite different from the other ascetics whom he used to meet in and around the temple. Though he too was dressed in saffron robe wrapped around his waist, like most other ascetics, this young man seemed very different, distinguished and well built. He had long and open hair, wore a garland of *rudraksh* beads on his neck (the holy beads worn by mendicants and ascetics), and wore *vibhuti basma* (sacred white ash) on his forehead.

nithyananda did not remember what the two of them talked about, except that the interaction left a profoundly blissful experience upon him. It also created a great longing in him to meet this young man again. As the young man was about to leave, nithyananda asked him whether he could see him again and if so, when. The young man said, 'Come here when ever you wish; call me if you wish to see and talk to me, and I shall come to you.'

nithyananda started coming to this place everyday without fail. Once he reached the *jiva samadhi*, he would call out, '*Swami, Swami*' and the young man would emerge smiling. nithyananda lost himself talking to him. It was as if he was a part of himself. He found himself filled with bliss and comfort. They talked for hours day after day. Since very few people came to this spot in the temple, they were left alone most of the time.

nithyananda asked the young man what his name was. The young man told him that his name was Arunagiri Yogiswara. Nithyananda at that time had no idea who Arunagiri Yogiswara was and did not recognize the name. Arunagiri Yogiswara became the hero, idol and inspiration to him. nithyananda was convinced that Arunagiri Yogiswara was what he wanted to be when he grew up. Everything about the young man was magnetic and enchanting.

nithyananda's attachment for the young man was so strong that he could not wait to see him in the mornings. He would rise very early in the mornings and leave home immediately for the temple and the *jiva samadhi*. When his mother became curious as to why he was leaving so early in the mornings, as nithyananda was never very fond of going to school, he gave her excuses saying that he had special classes to attend at school. What nithyananda felt with this young man was an indescribable joy of spirit.

Later on when talking to us, the Master described the experience he had with Arunagiri Yogiswara using the metaphor of two birds, from Mundaka Upanishad, an ancient Hindu scripture:

Two birds were sitting on a large fruit-bearing tree that had many branches. It had many fruits in each of its branches. One of the birds was a golden hued bird with a lovely plumage. It had a serene calmness about it and was perched silently upon one of the upper branches, which had fewer fruits. It spent most of its time unmoving, showing no interest in the fruits around it. The second bird was smaller and livelier; this bird was always restless and kept jumping from one branch to another branch searching for fruits to eat.

The second bird felt very happy when he tasted sweet fruits and chirped happily. When he came across a bitter or sour fruit which was often, he made irritated noises and looked unhappy. More the sour and bitter fruits that he tasted, more sorrowful this bird became. He said to himself that there was no joy in these fruits, there was no joy at all in living like this.

He then looked up and saw the blissful golden bird perched above him, sitting in silence, calm and relaxed. The golden bird seemed to light up the entire tree. The smaller bird flew up to look at the golden bird more closely. On the way up, he saw some juicy fruits and he stopped to peck at them. The fruits were tasty and he settled down to eat more. Then some fruits turned bitter, and some sour, and he grew disappointed. He looked up and saw the golden bird again, calm, happy, and relaxed. He moved up again.

He flitted up and down, right and left. Each time he saw the golden bird, he would fly up closer; he would then stop to taste a fruit that first tasted sweet, only to move on to bitter and sour fruits as he stayed on to eat more.

Finally, he reached the treetop where the golden bird was perched. He looked at him up close and was startled to find that the golden bird was none other than his own self. He went closer and closer, becoming happier and more relaxed. The smaller bird felt a deep connection with the golden hued bird. It was love; not falling in love, but rising in love. Soon he lost his own identity and merged with the golden bird.

nithyananda's feelings were similar though he could not have described his feelings with similar words as in the *Upanishad* at that time. It was his inner self-realizing that was his link with this person to whom he was attracted so strongly without any reason. It was as if he saw himself, his own Self, in the young stranger, who no longer seemed a stranger.

Arunagiri Yogiswara was the first person who helped nithyananda develop a conscious experience of himself. Through his discussions with him, he made nithyananda look beyond his exterior self. Even though he was still no more than a child, nithyananda felt the stirrings of the need to look within and explore deeper about his own existence, without quite knowing why and how.

nithyananda took to wandering all over the Arunachala hill with Arunagiri Yogiswara, who took him to places the boy had never been before. One day, they reached a point, which seemed a dead end, beyond which there seemed no path. However, as they continued to walk, a new path seemed to open up in front of them and they kept going further. In the distance, they saw a huge banyan tree. As they reached closer, they could see several older people seated under the tree.

nithyananda and Arunagiri Yogiswara reached the banyan tree and sat amongst the other people already assembled there. All of them greeted the young man deferentially and with love. Arunagiri Yogiswara introduced nithyananda to all the others and they all seemed very happy to meet this young man. All of them were dressed in saffron robes similar to what Arunagiri Yogiswara wore. All the older people sat around Arunagiri Yogiswara, who was far younger, and listened to him respectfully, as disciples would to a Master. To his surprise, nithyananda did not feel out of place here at all, amongst far older people and still being treated as an equal. For the first time, nithyananda felt the sheer beauty of the saffron robes and experienced a strong desire to wear one himself.

nithyananda asked Arunagiri Yogiswara whether he too could have a saffron robe to wear. Arunagiri Yogiswara gave the boy a saffron robe, similar to what all of them were wearing, and nithyananda put it on immediately. Nithyananda still preserves and treasures that saffron cloth that Arunagiri Yogiswara gave him that day, many years ago, under the banyan tree. This saffron robe, which is now at ashram in Bangalore, is proof that all that happened then was not a dream or a figment of the young boy's imagination, but the truth.

'What is this place, where are we?' he asked the young Master. Arunagiri Yogiswara said that this was his ashram, his home, the place where he taught. nithyananda then asked him, 'Then how do you manage to come so quickly, when I call you at the temple, at the burial place?' Arunagiri Yogiswara said, 'That is no problem, I can reach you fast.'

By evening that day, Arunagiri Yogiswara brought the boy back to the temple. nithyananda continued to see him every day. The boy did not feel that there was anything extraordinary or mysterious about this young man, who was a teacher to others and an ascetic, a *yogi*, who seemed to be on a spiritual pursuit. To nithyananda, Arunagiri Yogiswara was like any other ascetic, younger and one he could relate with comfortably. He took with him the saffron robe that he had given him, and carefully kept it with his clothes at home.

Some days later, nithyananda's mother saw the robe amongst his clothes and asked him about it; she wanted to know where he got it from and who gave it to him and why. nithyananda said that a young *yogi* who he met in the temple gave him the robe and she did not pursue the subject. A few days later nithyananda showed the robe to Kuppammal, his mentor. She too asked him about who gave him the robe. nithyananda responded saying that it was Arunagiri Yogiswara who have him the robe.

Kuppammal was taken aback. She retorted saying that Yogiswara would not give such a robe to nithyananda unless he were to accept the boy as a disciple. She then wanted to know how and where the boy had met him. nithyananda said he regularly met him near the burial place at the rear of the temple. Kuppammal felt that nithyananda was not telling her everything. She asked nithyananda to take her to the place and show her Arunagiri Yogiswara.

Innocently, nithyananda took her to the spot where he normally met Arunagiri Yogiswara and called out, '*Swami, Swami*'. However, there was no response this time. Normally he would come out as soon as he called him.

Kuppammal laughed at the boy's discomfiture. She asked, 'How will he come out? Where can he come out from? There is no place for anyone to stay here. Show me!'

The boy walked to the spot that Arunagiri Yogiswara normally came out from, which he had assumed was the entrance to a cave like enclosure. nithyananda was startled to find that there was no opening at all at that spot. There was only a stone slab there, covering whatever lay behind, and there was a figure sculpted on that stone slab. That figure looked uncannily like Arunagiri Yogiswara whom he used to meet every day.

Shocked, confused, and frightened, nithyananda started to cry. He had no idea what was happening. Kuppammal, contrary to her normal understanding and acceptance of whatever the boy said, would neither accept nor understand what he was trying to say. Perhaps she did understand but could not accept that she understood, or explain what was happening. nithyananda was weeping uncontrollably.

Kuppammal asked, 'How did he look? What did he do? Where did he take you? What did he say? How long have you been meeting him?'

nithyananda explained to her all that had happened. How Arunagiri Yogiswara had first appeared to him coming out of the burial place, how he had said that the boy could call him any time, how they used to meet every day, how he took him to various places, about the banyan tree, the elders around him and whatever he could remember of what they talked about.

Kuppammal burst out crying. She prostrated in front of that blocked cave entrance and started wailing: 'Master, so many people have been waiting to see you for so long! You never appeared. And yet you chose to play with this young boy now!'

nithyananda did not understand what Kuppammal was saying. He went away from the burial place into the temple in deep anguish and pain. He had lost someone, someone he felt very close to, something invaluable as a relationship, and he could not bear the thought of that loss. The boy missed his hero. He missed the *Yogi* not coming out as he called him. Most importantly, he could not understand why Arunagiri Yogiswara did not respond at all when he needed to prove to Kuppammal his identity, and to show her that he was speaking the truth. He felt betrayed.

As he went into the *garba graha* – the sanctum sanctorum - of the deity Arunachaleshwara, he saw the Arunagiri Yogiswara seated inside, on the Siva Linga; instead of the deity he saw him! He cried out, '*Swami! Swami*! you are here, why didn't you come when I called you at the *samadhi*? Kuppammal *Patti* (*patti* in Tamil means grandmother, an elderly woman) says you do not exist. She wants to see you.'

The *yogi* just sat there and smiled. The priests thought that the boy had lost his mind. They could not see Arunagiri Yogiswara, who the boy was talking to. They did not understand who the boy was talking to or why he was saying what he was saying. They pushed him out of the *garba graha*. The boy continued to shout, '*Swami*, please come out; please come out!'

nithyananda did not understand why the *Yogi* was not responding now, why he would not come out as he did before. He went home highly disturbed. It was an emotional roller coaster for him that night. At one level, he was at peace that he saw the *Yogi* in the *garba graha* smiling at him, that he had not lost him after all. At another level he was confused that he made no response.

The boy wondered what went wrong. Was he wrong in telling Kuppammal about the *Yogi*? Was it supposed to be a secret between the two of them, nithyananda and Arunagiri Yogiswara, that no one else was supposed to know about? Did he lose his friend through his carelessness, through his ignorant action? Was the *Yogi* angry with him? Will he never come back to see him?

It was a searing pain, pain of losing a part of himself; pain that he had not experienced before. He sobbed uncontrollably, tears pouring down his cheeks. nithyananda was mourning for a lost friend. The boy spent the whole night in agony. He thought that he would not wake up the next morning.

Early next morning, the boy ran to the spot where he used to call him. He sat in front of the *jiva samadhi* and wept. 'Why are you not coming out? Are you angry with me? If I have made a mistake, please forgive me. I cannot be without you, please come out and meet me, let me see you, please speak to me,' he cried.

Suddenly nithyananda saw Arunagiri Yogiswara in front of him, but in a very different form. Arunagiri Yogiswara was no longer flesh and blood, no longer in the physical form that the boy used to see him earlier. He was in a very different form. His whole form was in shining light, mystical and mysterious. Arunagiri Yogiswara's feet were not touching the ground. He was glowing, almost transparent.

Arunagiri Yogiswara smiled tenderly at the boy, full of compassion and love. He said, 'Dear one, you and I are one. We can never get separated. But the play is over. You will not miss me any longer. You will not be separated. We are one.'

Saying this, the form of Arunagiri Yogiswara merged into the boy and disappeared from his view. From that moment, nithyananda did not feel the separation and loss from Arunagiri Yogiswara at all.

It was as if Arunagiri Yogiswara was a part of him now. A deep fulfillment descended on him; complete bliss. It was an overflow of love, compassion, all positive emotions at their highest level.

Nithyananda says:

'This was probably my first moment of realization of who I really was. It was my first spiritual experience, my first moment of enlightenment. From that moment I stopped missing anything. All I missed from then on was only the idea of missing anything at all.'

It was only later that nithyananda realized that the person he played with, he related so closely with, this Arunagiri Yogiswara was none other than Arunachala, Siva Himself.

Many years later, at his ashram in Bidadi, Nithyananda met with Siva again! That experience will be described in a later part of His biography.

Nithyananda retains the saffron cloth that Siva gave him, with all its associated memories. nithyananda carried the cloth with him all through his *parivrajaka*, his wandering, through his *tapasya,* days of spiritual effort. The saffron is witness to the wonderful things that happened to his being at various stages in his life, from childhood, through his various stages of enlightenment.

On that day, nithyananda's childhood ended. nithyananda's walking, talking, and interaction with people became more mature, in line with the new realization, his enlightenment.

From that moment, a feeling of detachment, the feeling of just witnessing without involvement descended on nithyananda. There was detachment of what was happening around him, and a lack of any expectation of what needed to happen. A new consciousness started shining within him, which clearly indicated that whatever was happening around him was all-impermanent. Clarity in terms of what is eternal and what is ephemeral was expressed and experienced in his consciousness.

nithyananda stopped relating with his family as before and moved away from his friends as well. He felt comfortable relating only with a few people such as Kuppammal and similar spiritually advanced souls. He would often walk up on the Arunachala hill and sit on a rock; to just be with Arunachala. After this experience, he never felt that Arunachala was a hill, stone or statue; to him it was living energy.

Whenever nithyananda was in a temple procession, he would feel the nearness of his beloved Arunagiri Yogiswara. He would feel proud, like a child would, knowing that his father was an important person. This gave him an opportunity to re-experience the profound and powerful mystical experience that Arunagiri Yogiswara had bestowed upon him.

Nithyananda told us while recounting this incident, 'I got my body language from Arunagiri Yogishwar. He used to look like how I look now.'

The mystical banyan tree of Dakshinamurthy

Ramana Maharishi talks about a banyan tree that he visited once in the Arunachala hill. Ramana says that one day as he was walking on Arunachala hill, he was transported to this banyan tree and saw a young *Yogi* teaching far older disciples under that banyan tree. By implication, Ramana compared this tree and the *Yogi* he saw, to Lord Dakshinamurthy, incarnation of Siva Himself.

This is the same banyan tree that Sankara sang about in his *Dakshinamurthy Stotram*; under which the South-facing young boy taught older sages in silence. It is the same banyan tree that Ramana Maharishi spoke about.

Ramana said that no human being can go to that place by himself. Ramana then says that when he tried to go towards that location again another time, he stepped on a beehive and the angry bees attacked him. Ramana saw this as a sign that he was not to go to this place again and stopped. Later on, Ramana Maharishi's disciple Muruganar attempted to reach this banyan tree with a group of seekers. The entire group, who knew Arunachala hill well, ended up getting lost. Frightened, they gave up their attempt and returned.

Nithyananda says:

'When I see all these references to this banyan tree under which this young Master taught older disciples, as Arunagiri Yogiswara or Dakshinamurthy, I am convinced that they refer to *Shambhala*, abode of the *Sapta Rishis* (seven sages), the cosmic energy center.

One can reach Shambhala from Tapovan, which is over 17,500 feet in the Himalayas beyond Gangotri and Gomukh. With the Master's help one can reach Shambhala from anywhere. The enlightened master can act as an airstrip to take you to that space at any time. The airstrips from where you can fly to Shambhala are called energy fields. The banyan tree at Bidadi (Nithyananda's ashram outside Bangalore) is one such energy field to take off.

However, Shambhala is not on this earthly plane. Shambhala is an experience that is spiritual. That is what Ramana saw and I saw with Arunagiri Yogiswara. The tree that we both saw is the same banyan tree at Bidadi in our ashram.'

Appar, the great Tamil poet saint, sings in his ten verses long '*Kailaya Pathigam*' as to how he was transported to Kailash and saw Lord Siva and His Consort Parvati. Appar was not in Kailash in the physical plane when he had this spiritual experience. He was transported in spirit to this location, the abode of Gods.

The banyan tree that Ramana Maharishi refers to, and the banyan tree at Bidadi, are like airports or helipads to take off and reach the spiritual plane where Arunagiri Yogiswara resides in pure consciousness, as Dakshinamurthy, 'Siva' Himself.

nithyananda spent many years in the Himalayan regions and many months at Tapovan. From Gangotri, one has to trek to Gomukh first and from there climb to Tapovan. Tapovan has no access paths or any kind of shelter. At least in Gomukh, there is an ashram and some army tents. Tapovan has nothing, and no one. The ascetics, the *sanyasis*, the *yogis* who stay there have no protection from the elements, which can be life threatening, especially in the cruel winters. Traveling to and staying at Tapovan requires extensive acclimatization through extended periods of stay at lower levels at Gangotri and Gomukh.

Nithyananda when describing his stay at Tapovan, said that he stayed in caves and used jute bag material and paper to cover himself from the cold. He explained that Tapovan was the connection from the Earth, and the only connection from anywhere in our universe, to a non-physical location, an ethereal location, where the universal energy controlling the universe existed. Nithyananda says that this energy, this intelligence is what we refer to as God, divinity etc. and that this is the energy that enables the operation of this universe, which includes our planet Earth. The words *Shambhala*, as a reference to this Energy location and *Sapta Rishis,* or seven sages, to refer to the intelligent energy, as used by Nithyananda are metaphorical references to a non-physical location and non-physical entity. However, this location and this entity are very real.

In his 'Autobiography of a Yogi', *Paramahamsa* Yogananda describes the experiences of his Master, Yukteswar, with a similar non-physical location.

From our recent experiences with the Master, we know that there is very real danger of his spirit leaving his body when he reaches locations such as Gomukh and beyond. Even at lower levels of Gangotri, it is with very great difficulty that he had to stay out of *samadhi* state, when the spirit was no longer in its body frame. In 2004, when he traveled to Gomukh, he went into deep *samadhi* for many hours.

When talking about one of these experiences, the Master said even as he laughed: I was with the Energy at Shambhala. I told them that if they wished I would be very happy to stay on and not go back to my physical form. In seconds they threw me back into my physical body, much to the relief of the few close devotees around me at that time!

How enlightened Masters influence us even after they pass away

In his 'Autobiography of a Yogi', *Paramahamsa* Yogananda talks extensively about Mahavatar Baba, who even today walks in the Himalayan region. Baba who *Paramahamsa* Yogananda refers to and whom *Paramahamsa* Nithyananda met later in life, is available to all seekers. In fact, as we shall describe in a later part of this biography, a disciple of Nithyananda had a vision of Mahavatar Baba, when we toured the Himalayan region with the Master, in the summer of 2005, on the way to Kedarnath. Similarly, Arunagiri Yogiswara too is available to all seekers in planet Earth. He is Siva Himself.

This experience with Arunagiri Yogiswara created in young nithyananda a deep interest and thirst for the *advaitic* or non-dualistic experience. nithyananda's spiritual interests started with decorating and playing with idols of deities at a very early age. When he met the levitating *Yogi* he was introduced to extraordinary *yogic* experiences; with Kuppammal he was introduced to searching for knowledge; with Arunagiri Yogiswara he was for the first time exposed to an experience of consciousness, that enabled him to be aware of his inner Self. This event started in him a spiritual quest of a different dimension in the right direction.

After the experience with Arunagiri Yogiswara, nithyananda started spending more and more time at the *jiva samadhi.* The burial place of an enlightened Master's body is preserved and it continues to radiate energy. The body carries all memories. One cannot think without the body. Body is not mere matter as we think; and mind is not the only memory space as we think. Body and mind are both memories. If one can change memories, one can change the body. Memories of enlightened Masters are sharp, pure and powerful. Their bodies are buried to preserve these memories. Memories of ordinary people on the other hand are full of *samskara* and that's why their bodies are burnt so that these *samskara* do not haunt and disturb the living. As we mentioned elsewhere, this is the same reason why people feel the presence of unfriendly spirits in burial grounds.

Masters continuously respond to prayers of devotees even after their physical death, through their living energies. One can get an audience with them at their place of burial; relate to them and talk to them. Their telephone numbers are *mantras* relating to them! If one utters these *mantras* relating to the Master at his place of burial with awareness, there will be immediate connectivity in response to the prayer.

nithyananda started spending all his time at the burial place of Arunagiri Yogiswara. Earlier he used to skip school from time to time; now he stopped going to school altogether. The school Head Master complained to his parents. nithyananda's parents expressed their inability to do anything with their child to persuade him to go to school and told the Head Master to take care of it himself. The Head Master sent a security guard from the school to find and bring nithyananda to school. This security guard knew the boy's routine and would come to look for him at this place. nithyananda gave this old man whatever money he had with him and sent him away. As the man watched the boy spend all his time in meditation at the *jiva samadhi*, he became strangely attached to him and stopped bothering him. Instead of taking money from Nithyananda, he would bring him food and money, and altered the boy's attendance at school as well!

Nithyananda met this man, the security guard from his school, in 2004. The old man, much older now, dissolved into tears, remembering nostalgically the intense young child so deeply engrossed in his spiritual pursuit, and now a living enlightened Master.

Nithyananda says:

'There were many unconnected paradoxical illogical events that happened around this body. When these events are sought to be expressed in words, when they are attempted to be written down as facts, these events become lies. Spiritual experiences are multi-dimensional. Written words are two-dimensional, at best.

My biography cannot be a recording of all dimensions of the Truth. Written words cannot record all dimensions of the Truth, because Truth is much deeper than all written words. It is just a chronological recounting. Its purpose is to inspire. My experience with Arunagiri Yogiswara was even deeper than enlightenment. Enlightenment is an ultimate experience; it is not the final experience. It is the gateway to many more spiritual experiences.'

Background Information on the story of two birds from: Mundaka Upanishad

THIRD MUNDAKA FIRST KHANDA

द्वा सुपर्ण सयुजा सखाया समानं वृक्षं परिषस्वजाते तयोरन्य:
पिप्पलं स्वाद्वत्त्यनश्नन्नन्यो अभीचाकशीति ।।१।।

समाने वृक्षे पुरुषो निमग्नोऽनीशया शोचति मुह्यमान: । जुष्टं
यदा पश्यत्यन्यमीशमस्य महिमानमिति वीतशोक: ।।२।।

Two birds living together, each the friend of the other, perch upon the same tree. Of these two, one eats the sweet fruit of the tree, but the other simply looks on without eating.

The two birds are the *Jiva* (*Atman*) and *Iswara* (*Brahman*) both existing in an individual compared to a tree. They exist together as the reflection and the original. They both manifest themselves in different ways in every individual. From the characteristics of the *Jiva*, it is possible to infer the nature of *Iswara* and from the nature of *Iswara* it is possible to determine the potentialities of the *Jiva*. Both the *Jiva* and *Iswara* have a common substratum which is Brahman and which is the reality of both. The body is compared to a tree, because it can be cut down like a tree. This tree is also called the *Kshetra* or the field of manifestation and action of the *Kshetrajna* or the knower of the field. The body is the field of action and experience and it is the fruit of actions done already.

That which distinguishes the *Jiva* from *Iswara* is the mind only. In fact, the mind itself constitutes the *Jiva*. It is the *Jiva* that is affected by *Avidya*, *Kama* and *Karma*. Because of the conjunction of consciousness with these limiting factors, it has to experience the results of its actions; but *Iswara* who is not limited to any adjunct, has no actions whatsoever to perform and so, no experience of the results of actions.

The fruits enjoyed by the *Jiva* are of the nature of pleasure and pain, i.e., they are all relative experiences born of non-discrimination. The experience of *Iswara* is eternal and is of the nature of purity, knowledge and freedom. Relative experience is the effect of the presence of *Rajas*, but the character of *Iswara* is *Sattva* (the highest state of calmness and detachment denoting a state of spiritual evolution), and hence, there is no phenomenal experience for Him. He is in fact the director of both the agent of actions and the results of actions, *Iswara's* activity consists in His mere existence. The value of His existence is greater than that of the activity of the whole universe. It is His existence that actuates the whole universe of manifestation.

In the same tree, the individual (bird) is drowned in grief because of delusion and impotency. When it beholds the other (bird), viz., the adorable Lord, it realizes its own glory and gets freed from sorrow.

The grief of the *Jiva* is the result of its inability to live in conformity with the forms of the effects of unwise actions done in the past. Such thoughtless actions, no doubt, lead to their corresponding results and as they are not in tune with the law of Truth; they torment the individual in the form of unpleasant experiences. Without a relative experience, the individual cannot live and with every relative experience produced by lack of wisdom, fresh misery is added to the pre-existing lot.

Thus, from the highest standpoint, the entirety of the experience of the individual consists of grief alone. Because of its confinement to the forms of its desires and actions, the *Jiva* feels itself to be impotent, confused and helpless.

It is even made to feel that a particular experience to which it is connected is alone real and that there is no reality beyond it. Due to this, it is now and then connected with and separated from the objects of its desire. It is born and it dies, passing through several kinds of wombs in accordance with the kinds of its actions.

The freedom of the individual consists in the vision of the Lord Supreme, Who is co-existent with it, in fact inseparable from it as its very Self. The realization of *Iswara* is the same as the raising of the individual consciousness to the consciousness of *Iswara*. The *Jiva* ceases to exist the moment it realizes *Iswara*. The glory of the real essence of the individual is known only when the veil covering it, is removed. This is achieved in the realization of God. The ultimate realization is in the form of the identity of the Self with the Supreme Being. Here, the whole universe is realized to be the same as the essence of the spiritual infinite. This realization puts an end to all kinds of imperfections and sorrows.

(The above is based on translation of *The Mundaka Upanishad* by Swami Krishnananda of The Divine Life Society, Sivananda Ashram, Rishikesh, India)

Chapter - 6

First Spiritual Awakening

Choicelessness is an attribute of enlightened beings

Even incarnations need to be provided with the right ambience as they grow in their earthly bodies.

Saradananda says in Ramakrishna's biography:

Does the unbroken memory of previous enlightened births exist in an incarnation from his very childhood?

The authors of the Puranas reply: Although it is always latent within the incarnation, these memories do not always manifest themselves in childhood. However, as the avatar's mind-body organism becomes mature, his memory awakens with little or no effort.

The ambience of upbringing needs to be supportive and conducive for the effectiveness of their mission. The Divine Existence, the *Parasakti*, plans their process of settling down on planet Earth in line with the mission it has determined for them. Events appear to happen at random, but are never really random. There is a correlation between one event and another, and the sequence, the path, is almost preordained.

Ironically, and very different from how many of us perceive this, we ordinary mortals have definitive free will in choosing our paths. We all encounter many forks as we traverse the path of life, and it is for us to choose the fork we wish to travel by. Depending on what and how we choose, events unfold accordingly.

In the case of enlightened beings, there is an element of choicelessness that is part of the divine package. They just move with the will of the universe in a total spirit of no-mind and surrender. Because of this, all their desires, even as they spring from their causal layer, are immediately fulfilled. We see that every word they utter is true and becomes true.

Those who have been with Nithyananda, know very well that when He says after listening to some one's problem, 'I will take care', that issue is immediately resolved. All the Master does, He says, is to hand over the problem to *Parasakti*, the universal Mother, to take care, and she does.

When incarnations such as Nithyananda reach planet Earth, they are without *samskara* and are at the doorstep of enlightenment. They have to let go the tiny element of *satvic guna* - the highest state of calmness and detachment denoting a state of spiritual evolution - that they are born with to reach enlightenment.

Enlightenment happens; it cannot be made to happen. Enlightenment is like river water. It stays in your hands as long as your hands are open; once you close your hands to possess it, there is nothing to hold.

Nithyananda says we are all enlightened; we are all born with divinity within ourselves. It is the awareness of this divinity within us that is missing in most of us. 'The only difference between you and I,' He says, 'is that I know I am divine, and you as yet do not know.' Since that truth already exists in us, we cannot achieve it; we just need to become aware of it, that's all.

Bliss, the outcome of this awareness, enlightenment, is choicelessness. If we try to make bliss a choice, it will be absent. If we can understand the purposelessness of life as a part of the grand plan of Existence, we *can* and *will* reach enlightenment and experience bliss.

Our ego believes that there is purpose to life - material, relational and spiritual. The more the purposes to work towards, the stronger our ego feels. If we drop all other purposes and still hold on to the purpose of enlightenment, it is futile. Only when we realize that life is totally purposeless and drop our ego, will enlightenment happen to us.

Even logically, what is the purpose of existence? God who creates everything else including jungles, could he not have created concrete jungles and cities as well? The only purpose of existence is bliss, that's all.

How can we enjoy without possessing, without making something our own? We are like water bubbles on a wave in the ocean. But what happens is, each bubble catches hold of a few more bubbles calling them wife, husband, father, and son. It collects pieces of sand, thinking they are jewels. The bubble does not understand that it can burst any moment. Suddenly one big bubble says, it is going to be enlightened. This is what happens in us.

When we are ready to digest the truth that everything is purposeless, material, relational, spiritual, only then life acquires meaning. Once we have a goal we miss the path.

The mind waits for something to happen. It waits for salary, weekly, monthly, yearly, and 5 yearly payments. If someone offers us 100 years of salary and asks us to die tomorrow, will we die? When we measure life by paycheck, we reduce our spirit to matter.

Our ego is stuck on what we see as a purpose in life. We say, 'After I settle my social responsibilities, I will come to you, my Master, and take up the spiritual path.'

An elderly lady came to Nithyananda with her son and wanted him to take the son into the ashram as a *brahmachari*, a student in spiritual studies. Nithyananda was surprised, since usually no parent wants their child to be a *sanyasi*. Vivekananda is great and is admired, but no one wants his own son to be a Vivekananda. They wonder how their son or daughter can be so blissful, when they have not experienced such bliss themselves.

Nithyananda asked her why she wanted her son to be at the ashram. She said that her son was mentally unsound.

Nithyananda retorted: *Amma*, I am running an ashram, not an asylum!

We have many reasons why we cannot do things. By the time we finish one responsibility, we have ten more waiting for us. Running becomes our conditioning; we don't know how to relax. When we are young, we tell ourselves that we will relax after we graduate from university; then we shift the goal post to marriage; then to children; then to educating children; then their marriage. By the time we are 60, we have missed the path itself! Where is the question of enjoying?

The primal sin that we can commit is, miss the path of life by following goals. When we live, let our being be blissful; when we start hurrying, let us think about what we are hurrying for; let us not allow restlessness in us, hoping that it will settle; that will never happen. If we are not able to relax into the present moment, even after fulfilling our responsibilities, we will still feel unfulfilled. Whenever we run, whenever we hurry, let us ask 'why', 'what for'?

We may have big houses, drive big cars, and have people around us always praising us. Can we carry anything of these with us? Can we carry with us even one single checkbook when we die? It is all purposeless.

When we understand this purposelessness, healing happens. Even if we have been abused, we will heal; if we allow this understanding to happen, the understanding itself will guide us.

'What kind of teaching is this,' one may ask. 'All my life I have had a purpose, and my life has been fine. Now you say all that is without purpose.' Whether we like it or not, that is the truth.

Our seeing an enlightened Master is a dream. Scriptures say: The moment one **sees** an enlightened Master, one becomes enlightened.

Seeing the Master is not the same as looking at him, which is what we do. *Looking* is with our eyes, **seeing** is with the Being. The closer we come to the Master, the more our understanding of him changes. Our maturity allows us to see him differently.

Purposelessness does not mean saying, 'Now I know life is purposeless. I don't want to go to work. I don't want to take a vacation.' This is a wrong understanding. Once you have the understanding of purposelessness, you can never be lazy. *Tamas* (laziness) will never come out of intelligence. Perhaps for two days you will just lie in bed and not get up. On the third day, you will wake up as a different person, without restlessness. Restlessness is a monster that one conquers when one understands the real purposelessness of life.

Restlessness hides purposelessness from us; it hides the path with the goal. If this is understood, we will be healed. All our dreams of the future, all our guilt of the past will disappear; all ephemeral joys and suffering will vanish.

We referred earlier to the saint in Tiruvannamalai, Visiri Swamigal or Yogi Ram Surat Kumar. He was innocent as a child. Whenever people came to him, whatever their problem was, he would say 'alright'. If someone said, 'Someone died Swami,' he would say 'alright'; If someone said, 'My son is getting married Swami,' he would say 'alright'.

One day, nithyananda asked him, 'Swami, why do you say alright to everything?' He replied, 'Everything is just purposeless. Whatever you think has a purpose has no meaning; so it is alright.' Whenever we remember the truth of purposelessness, healing will happen, suffering will disappear; whether we have or do not have, neither has purpose.

We need courage to pursue the Truth and be enlightened. Life will then take a different path. We will live as liberated souls. We will never drop our jobs, our relationships or our wealth. We will drop only what we do not have. We will drop the mental associations and emotions attached to objects and events. We will drop the fantasy of a throne and start enjoying the seat. Status will no longer have meaning; one's own inner state will be all that matters.

When purpose is dropped, the real meaning will happen.

nithyananda's path to enlightenment had its own challenges. As is narrated later, his first spiritual experience occurred when he was barely twelve. However, it took another 10 years before enlightenment happened to him. Nithyananda says now that had he let go, possibly it would have happened earlier. His own struggles and rigorous practices perhaps delayed what may have happened sooner.

Kuppammal, the neighborhood Guru, takes charge

When nithyananda was around seven and was at the *Devi sannadi* (altar of Goddess Parvati) of the Arunachaleshwara temple one day, he suddenly had a vision of a golden colored figure. The figure made such an impression on him that he felt impelled to draw it immediately. He got himself a copper sheet and a nail and started carving this diagram out of memory.

When nithyananda's grandmother saw him engaged in this work, she became curious and wanted to know what he was doing and what this figure was. nithyananda told her that he was drawing something he saw in his mind. She was not satisfied with this explanation. Unsure of what her grandson was up to, she asked her friend Kuppammal for advice.

Kuppammal, who was known as Brahmayogini Vibhudhananda Devi Maataji Kuppammal, was a sincere spiritual seeker. Kuppammal's mother was without a child for a long time. The mother's guru was Seshadri Swamigal, an enlightened Master of great reputation in Tiruvannamalai, and a contemporary of Ramana Maharishi. Seshadri Swamigal blessed the lady and gave her a handful of mud to eat. With complete faith and no hesitation, the lady ate all of it. Later that year, Kuppammal was born, as if by divine providence.

Kuppammal had mastered the art of *Kundalini tantra* by the age of 12. She never menstruated till she was 21. Against her will, she was married off by the time she was nineteen and was stopped from doing her spiritual practices. Only after her marriage, about two years after she stopped her practices, she started menstruating.

She was deeply involved with the *Tiruppugazh Maadar Sangam* – a small movement to spread great Tamil literary works like Tiruppugazh etc. Kuppammal was adept in *tantric* practices and could materialize anything she wanted. She had the vision of Goddess Parvati as Raja Rajeshwari. She became a great inspiration and a compassionate guide to young nithyananda. She added much into molding his personality.

Kuppammal asked nithyananda how he came to draw this figure and he told her what happened. She explained to him that what he had drawn was the very powerful *Sri Chakra*, a highly complex and metaphorical representation of the universal energy, which even very highly trained artists found difficult to draw. She was astounded that the young boy had so casually drawn the figure from memory. (Years later, our Master Nithyananda drew this chakra on a blackboard in order to explain its meaning). Kuppammal asked nithyananda whether he would like to learn the science of *tantra*, which used the *Sri Chakra* as a base for meditation practices, and the boy eagerly accepted this offer.

Kuppammal was the first person who made nithyananda realize that he was different from other children of his age; that there was something extraordinary in his life. Till then nithyananda had not realized that what was happening to him was unlike whatever any one else around him was experiencing.

Kuppammal spent hours on end talking to the young boy and led him from devotion into meditation, from *bhakti* (devotion) into *jnana* (wisdom) and *dhyana* (meditation), with the help of her own Master, Isakki Swamigal. She regretted her marriage, and single-mindedly focused on her spiritual pursuit. Isakki Swamigal contributed to nithyananda's growing years by presenting him a book *Atma Purana* - a collection of material from the *Upanishad* which offers one a deep conviction of the all pervading existential energy. This book, as well as a protective verse, a *kaappu* in Tamil, and a conch given by Isakki Swami through Kuppammal are in the archives in the Bangalore ashram today.

Isakki Swamigal was an *avadhoot*, who never wore any clothes. Kuppammal gave the boy many books and predicted that he would keep these books till he himself started providing commentaries on them based on his wisdom. Nithyananda recalls that he used to spend hours reading from *Atma Purana*, which was written in Tamil as a collection of scriptural material from various Upanishad, sitting in front of Isakki Swamigal and Kuppammal. Kuppammal would explain what he read and from time to time Isakki Swamigal would comment and correct as needed. *Atma Purana* was the first book on Vedanta that nithyananda was exposed to.

Primal fear on being attacked by Hyenas

nithyananda used to walk around the Arunachala mountain every day around this period of his childhood, when he was not yet ten. He would start very early in the morning, at around 4 am, and walk for three to four hours around the hill, chanting songs while walking. nithyananda was totally in the present, least bothered about what was going to happen the next moment - like an innocent child playing in the lap of his mother; an innocent child delighting in the ambience of his beloved Arunachala.

One morning he started very early, soon after midnight. In those days there were no roads, nor lights on the path around the hill. It was just a jungle, a dense forest all the way. At a spot near *Sona Nadi*, a rivulet, a herd of hyenas approached him.

nithyananda had been walking with his eyes cast downwards singing devotional songs. He was totally immersed in singing and did not notice the hyenas till he was very close to them. When he lifted his head and saw them, the animals were ready to pounce on him.

From deep down his *hara,* the *Swadishthana chakra* or spleen energy center point, the boy let out a scream in desperate fear. It was a scream of pure fear that he had experienced neither before nor after. Along with the scream he felt a total surrender to Arunachala, and a deep trust that Arunachala would take care of him. Suddenly, an elderly *sanyasi* appeared in front of him from nowhere, with a big stick, and chased away the hyenas. As soon as the animals ran away, the old man disappeared. nithyananda did not know where this man came from, nor where he went.

With that primal scream, nithyananda found that his body had suddenly turned much lighter; he started walking, almost floating as if the frequency of his being had increased. (Primal theory is a modern psychological treatment in which patients scream from deep down their *hara,* to relieve fear and other suppressed negative emotions in catharsis).

In later days, Nithyananda often told us about the need to surrender completely to Existence, without any trace of ego, with the absolute confidence that Existence will take care of us in any eventuality. This incident is another of his own experiences even before his enlightenment, when sheer trust in Existence took care of what needed to be done.

Meeting Rudraksha Muni

nithyananda had heard of a sage whom people called Rudraksha Muni, who used to come to the Arunachaleshwara temple at night and occupy a place near the Rudraksha Mandapam. For many days, nithyananda waited for him at this spot without success. One night, a man covered with *rudraksh* appeared in the temple. (*Rudraksh* is the seed of a plant and is considered to be holy and capable of storing the existential energy in it.) Taking him to be Rudraksha Muni, nithyananda ran after him. nithyananda followed this man's schedule everyday and waited to serve him and talk to him.

One day he followed the man as he left the temple and found him walking into a house not far from the temple. He had a family and children! nithyananda was angry and felt cheated. He accosted the man and asked him why he didn't tell him that he was not Rudraksha Muni.

This man was a kind man. He explained to nithyananda that seeing how keen he was to meet Rudraksha Muni, and how disappointed he would be in not meeting him, he decided to play along so as not to disappoint him! He said, 'You were so joyful that you had met Rudraksha Muni. I could not take away that joy from you. I too felt so much joy with you around.'

Over time this man became a good friend. He was a depressed man seeking spiritual solace. He gave nithyananda a whole bagful of *rudraksh mala* (*rudraksh* strung into chains) that feature in some of the early photographs of nithyananda.

At this age, nithyananda was already quite knowledgeable about Hindu scriptures and epics, not only in terms of a mere story line but the inner meaning as well. He used to frequent all spiritual discourses in Tiruvannamalai and ask penetrating questions. On many occasions the speakers had problems in answering this young lad, and one speaker in fact told the organizers that if the young lad asked any more questions, he would be forced to stop his speech and leave. The same way as Ramakrishna *Paramahamsa* used to do in childhood, nithyananda too stood up to question the scholars who were merely intellectual without experience and offer more clarity to those who truly were.

On one occasion, Kripananda Variar, a very learned and famous spiritual guru who used to deliver lectures, came to Tiruvannamalai. During the discourse, he said in Tamil, '*angam veru lingam veru aagakoodaadu*', meaning that those who wear a *Siva linga* as a necklace on their body should never remove it, or rather should never be separate from it at any time. Young nithyananda asked him: 'Even the most intelligent man is bound to separate it, when he removes it to change the string. What you are implying is, when you become one with God, when you have realized God within, you and the *linga* within you cannot be separated, you and the God within you can never be separated. That is what you mean. You are talking about enlightenment; you are actually referring to the inherent state of an enlightened person, how *one* he has become with God, because of which he can never be separate from Him at any moment. How then can you make this statement as a technique to ordinary men?'

Kripaananda Variyar could have given any intellectual reply to nithyananda and silenced him but he did not do that. He immediately accepted with graciousness, what the boy said, and told him he was absolutely correct.

At the end of the discourse, as the boy went to pay his respects to him, he told him, '*appa, avvaykku Murugan madiri nee enakku vandu vazhi kattinai.* It means, 'dear one, like Murugan Himself showed His devotee saint Avvaiyar, you came to show me the way.' He went on to say that like how Lord Muruga as a child stunned Avvaiyar (a lady enlightened Master) with a certain question of his and made Her surrender Her ego instantaneously, the young boy had asked him a question and shaken him. In that incident, Variyar stood out for his humility.

Nithyananda still remembers this incident with deep affection for this wonderful person, who despite all his scholarship and age, had no qualms in accepting that the young boy was right, that too in public. He later told us that life was continuously teaching him through someone, through something, at every passing phase. People simply came and went touching him at the appropriate times in his quest.

Annamalai Swamigal and the self inflicted wound

Whenever he could, nithyananda would spend time cleaning the idols of the various deities in the Arunachala temple. By now, he had a group of young followers who would do what he told them to. They would go around cleaning and decorating the idols and organizing small events. A lady doctor, who used to be a family friend, recalls that when nithyananda came across a deity uncared for and a temple unattended, he used to shed tears and immediately get to work on cleaning up the place.

Around the age of 10, nithyananda started going to the Ramana Ashram in Tiruvannamalai. He was initially taken there by a relative, and then he started visiting the ashram by himself. He would spend hours in the ashram meditating and reading books from the ashram library. On one of these occasions, a family member took him to meet Annamalai Swamigal, an elderly man who was an enlightened disciple of Ramana Maharishi. nithyananda took to sitting with Annamalai Swamigal's disciples regularly.

nithyananda says that one of the attractions of going to Annamalai Swamigal was that he used to distribute candies after his discourses which young nithyananda loved! Annamalai Swamigal was a master of the *advaita* philosophy of non-duality. In *Advaita* philosophy, there is no separation between individual and divinity; both are one, there is no separation. It is our ignorance in the form of illusion or *maya* that prevents us from realizing we too are divine, that we too are in God's form.

One day, in the discourse, nithyananda heard Annamalai Swamigal explaining the concept of *maya* or illusion, when he said, 'We are not the body; this body is not real; what is real is the spirit; there is no pain that can affect this spirit; we are beyond pain and suffering.'

The concept of *maya* is quite fundamental to the *Advaita* concept of Sankara and the principles of *Vedanta* philosophy propounded by him. *Vedanta* literally means the end of knowledge and in that sense seeks to explain all that there is to know about the truth of life. Sages like Ramana and his followers such as Annamalai Swamigal explained the Ultimate Truth about the divinity of the individual through an elaboration of the concept of *maya* or illusion.

Ya ma, iti maya, say the scriptures. It means, 'that which is not real is *maya*'; *maya* is loosely translated in English as 'illusion'. We all see what we wish to see, not what there is as reality around us. We are all driven by our mind, our thoughts, or desires. We live in a fantasy world that we create around ourselves.

The *Upanishad* say:

As our thoughts are, so are our desires; as our desires are, so is our will; as our will is, so are our actions; as our actions are, so are our lives destined.

We are driven by our desires. These desires in the form of thoughts are our connectivity between the past and the future. We constantly seek to relive our past as it was, if it was enjoyable or as it should have been, if it was not enjoyable. The past cannot be recreated. Neither the past nor the future is real. One is dead and gone, never to return, and the other yet to come, quite speculative. Neither really matters, if you deeply think about it. There is nothing one can do about either, that would make any difference. We cannot change the past, and we cannot influence the future, however much we believe we can.

Even those of us who are full of our own confidence in how we shape our future, will realize the futility of what we believe in, when we realize that we do not even know whether we shall live to breathe our next breath. Even this simple action is not under our control. Yet we believe that we control and can control our future. The fact that we have free will and can decide what action we can take next has no bearing what so ever on the fact of our ability to shape our future. We can define our present and we should; that is all we can and should do. The future takes care of itself.

Yet, our mind is constantly focused on the past and the future, caught in the web of dilemma between these two. Our mind would like to interpret everything based on the unreality of what has happened in the past and what it would like to happen in the future. We love to live with dilemmas.
If for a moment, we could suspend desires and thoughts, if only we could disengage our minds, we would be in the present. We would be where reality is, where life is, where Bliss is. Being in the present, being in the here and now guarantees that we are grounded in reality, free from *maya.* In this state, we see life as it is, not as we want it to be.

In this state of the present, there are no expectations, as we take things as they are, as they come; there are no attachments as there are no expectations; there are no emotional attachments and we are light in the Being; there are no unfulfilled desires, no *samskara* any more, and we are close to the awareness of enlightenment.

Because there are no attachments in the present, there is no suffering. This is what Buddha referred to, when he said that desires cause suffering; that the attachment to what we want, the hangover of our desires, causes suffering. Mindfulness, the ability to be in the present, eliminates suffering.

When Annamalai Swamigal said that there would be no pain, he referred to the suffering attached to the physical pain. Pain in purely physical terms is bearable; it is the emotional suffering that is attached to the pain that causes us great discomfort.

Normally you may be fascinated by a concept that seems very attractive, especially if it is something very different from what you normally experience. However, you are still stuck with the reality of your experience and your mind points out that the concept is unrealistic. Unless you question both the concept and your mind's response, you will not realize the truth.

This attitude of questioning without pre-knowledge and without ego is the attitude of the true seeker. Only a true seeker is not content with reality as it is presented to him; a true seeker is also not ready to accept a concept however beguiling it may be; he is impelled to question both. He would question, and continue questioning the logic of the conclusion till he is satisfied. He will doubt reality and keep doubting reality till he goes beyond the superficiality of his perceptions, and he understands the truth by his own experience.

However, mostly we tend to question based on existing knowledge. Questions arise to show that we know. These types of questions are violent; only intent being to prove the inferior knowledge of another person. Such questions breed more questions as they are answered, not from a seeking perspective, but from the attitude of not wishing to accept another's knowledge.

nithyananda's questions were more in the nature of doubts that arose from an attitude of establishing truth, from the curiosity of a child, and not from the arrogance of an adult.

Nithyananda says:

When your ego drops, you will no longer have questions, only doubts. Doubts reflect the faith you have in the person you question. Questions reflect your own internal arrogance.

Despite his age and lack of experience, at a very deep level, nithyananda understood what Annamalai Swamigal said. He knew it was true, at his Being level. However, he needed to experience that truth as he understood it. Then and only then would it have been his truth, his reality. 'If I am the spirit and not the body alone, then the pain should not affect me; let me test this out,' determined the young lad.

nithyananda could not sleep that night. Annamalai Swamigal's words haunted him. The vibration of his presence and the piercing gaze of this enlightened Master stayed with him. He needed to prove for himself the correctness of what this Master had said in passing.

He thought to himself: 'Even though the conclusion that pain and suffering do not exist is fascinating, reality is different. I do and others do feel pain when we are hurt. It is indeed a fascinating conclusion that my body will not have pain and suffering; but this is different from my experience of reality. Therefore, I would need to test this out.'

When he woke up the next morning, nithyananda took a knife from his mother's kitchen and cut himself on his thigh, just below the pair of shorts he was wearing. It was a deep cut and started bleeding profusely. nithyananda was in deep pain but stopped short of crying out for fear of attracting too much attention. He was also confused when the wound caused him pain, as he expected that there would be no pain. Unable to bear the pain after a few minutes, he went to his mother, who immediately rushed him to a doctor who lived nearby. The doctor stitched his cut, his mother spanked him and the pain stayed for a while. The scar still remains on his thigh.

Later that day, nithyananda went to Annamalai Swamigal and told him what happened. He demanded, 'You said this body is not real; pain is not real; there will be no pain and suffering. But there was pain when I cut myself. Not only was there physical pain, but I also had the suffering of being spanked by my mother. Why?'
Annamalai Swamigal laughed and said, 'But I did not ask you to cut yourself to test what I said. Why did you do that?'

Annamalai Swamigal understood the seriousness of the boy's seeking; he was willing to undergo tremendous pain and suffering to test out a concept that he had understood as an intellectual truth. He decided to help the boy in his search, and asked him whether he would be prepared to follow a simple technique that would help him in his spiritual quest. nithyananda immediately accepted the offer. Annamalai Swamigal explained to nithyananda in greater detail about body, mind and spirit, and taught him a simple meditation technique to follow his thoughts back to the source where they originated.

nithyananda asked him, 'Swami, why did you not teach me this earlier? I need not have cut myself to learn this. I need not have experienced pain and suffering.'

Annamalai Swamigal said, 'Son, do not worry about this pain. It shall pass. You had the courage to test the truth and find out for yourself. That's the true sign of a seeker. Your courage will liberate you. It is far more valuable than the pain.'

These words stayed forever in nithyananda's mind. They initiated a transformation in him. These words remained a source of strength to support him whenever doubts assailed him as to whether the path he was following was the right one. It was an inspiration to run faster.

This experience of the self inflicted wound as a result of Annamalai Swamigal's teaching and the meditation that he initiated him into, started yet another new chapter in nithyananda's life. This experience helped him to go beyond the illusion of thoughts directly into the source of thoughts.

The attributes of what is seen as the object, the process of seeing and the seer as the subject are all thoughts at different levels of frequencies. First person is the subject or *seer*, third person is the object that is *seen*, and what is in between is the process of *seeing*. When nithyananda started going to the source of thoughts, he realized that all these three were same, only different levels of illusion created by his own thoughts. Going back to the source of thoughts was to go right into the present moment. At the 'present' moment, there is only the reality of 'being', nothing else. The activity of 'being' is the experience that encompasses the experiencer as well as the experienced.

In his *Atma Shatakam*, Sankara says beautifully:

Aham bhojanam naiva bhojyam na bhokta, shivoham shivoham
I am not the enjoyment, I am not the enjoyed, nor the enjoyer; I am beyond all three; I am the Truth.

nithyananda realized that the ultimate reality was to go beyond these thoughts right back to their source to a state of no mind. He developed the habit of sitting by himself and practicing the technique that Annamalai Swamigal had taught, more as a play than any serious meditation.

'Just sitting, just being had become a habit with me,' He later told us.

Spiritual awakening

nithyananda practiced the technique that Annamalai Swamigal had taught him with all commitment and discipline. Swamigal had told him, 'Practice this meditation and you will get your answers', and he was desperate to get to the answers.

A little over a year later, when nithyananda was about twelve, he was as usual sitting on a rock locally called
Pavazha Kunru (Pearl Rock) in the Arunachala hill and meditating, actually playing with this technique given to him, when a strange

experience happened. It was on the *Buddha Purnima* day (full moon day) in the month of *Vaikasi* (May-June as per the Tamil calendar), and evening sunset period.

In the midst of his meditation, nithyananda felt something opening up within him, something was getting crushed, something else was getting created. It was like a vessel inside getting broken and a door opening, both together at the same time. It was a feeling of creation and destruction at the same time; and a very pleasurable feeling. A feeling of calmness descended on him.

Even with his eyes closed, he could see all around him. He did not need his eyes to be open to see. Not just that, he had a 360-degree vision with his eyes closed. With equal clarity, nithyananda could see the hill in front of him, the temple behind him, the rock below him, the stars above him, the trees to the left, part of the hill to the right, all these were in his visionary field, without having to open his eyes!

Nithyananda says,

'At that moment, I awakened to the realization that I was one with the whole of Existence and everything was I!' He said pointing to the tree in front of him, 'It was like this tree became my bone and this thatch above became my nerves!'

nithyananda stayed in this state for over an hour and a half. He returned home drunk with excitement and told Kuppammal about what had happened. Kuppammal immediately knew that the boy had had a very powerful spiritual experience, very unusual for a person of his age and that he needed to be looked after. She took very good care of him. The after-effects of this spiritual experience that Nithyananda now calls *satori,* lasted about three days. (*satori* in the Japanese Zen context means enlightenment).

This *satori* experience was the beginning of a new phase of spiritual development in nithyananda's life.

From this point, nithyananda could see all around him when he wished. He called a close friend of his called Sampath soon after the *satori* incident, took him inside the temple with him and sat with him with his back to a tree. 'Look here,' he told his friend, 'something strange has happened to me. I can now see all around me.' His friend looked at him without comprehension.

He told his friend who was seated in front of him, 'Look at the tree behind me. Can you see the ant which is moving at this point?' and signaled to the spot behind him where an ant was indeed moving. nithyananda made his friend place coins and objects behind his head and was able to identify them correctly. nithyananda's friend was frightened at what was happening and ran away under the pretext of wanting to drink some water. This friend later told nithyananda's parents what nithyananda had shown him.

Nithyananda now refers to this experience as a glimpse of enlightenment and uses the Japanese Zen word *satori* to describe it. In the case of persons with whom we have seen this experience happen within the follower group, it is an experience that seems to happen in the presence of the Master with the grace of the Master. In the case of nithyananda, it happened on its own, partly out of the spiritual practice he was undergoing, and mainly as a result of his own evolved state.

Nithyananda asked one of his disciples once, why he was not doing his meditation as rigorously as it should have been practiced. He further told him, 'If I had been lazy like you, I would never have been enlightened.' The disciple responded tongue in cheek, 'That's because you did not have a Master like we have! We are far more fortunate than you!!'

Nithyananda himself says that had he surrendered to a Master, his own spiritual growth may have been faster. He says that he had to experiment with ten thousand keys before he could find the right key that unlocked the mystery of enlightenment. He says that in the case of his disciples, he has already given them the keys and all that they have to do is to fit the key to the lock for the Truth to dawn. From this time onwards, from this profound incident, nithyananda found that he could not balance himself on a cycle or a two-wheeler.

There was no sense of balance in the body. His elder brother used to ride him pillion on his cycle to school and back. Both his brothers used to laughingly complain about having to pedal his weight everyday. When he was refused a ride, nithyananda would walk. Nithyananda later recalled to us, 'Children of that age, at least out of peer pressure would have attempted to ride a bicycle, but I held on to my inability so adamantly and allowed things to take their own course, walking if need be miles together to where I had to reach, if I wasn't given a ride.'

He could not also wear any tight fitting clothes after this profound experience. He found that any clothing that separated his lower body from the upper, caused him discomfort. He would wear loose fitting clothes and pull it over his waist string.

Nithyananda recalled to a group of us one day, the hilarious consequences that followed due to not being able to ride a bicycle:

My older brother used to take me by bicycle everyday to school. On my way to school and on return, I would stop by at every temple and offer worship. He used to curse me saying that it was bad enough he had to pedal me to school, I also made him stop at every temple on the way as well!

By the time I visited these temples and reached school, it would be almost time to return. I was perpetually late. I used to mark my attendance with all the deities and then only go to school. At every temple, I would prostrate before each and every deity and then only leave the temple. I had a special and long mantra for each deity. If I missed this morning routine due to some urgent work, I would recite the mantras twice the next time, to make up for the lost day, fearing that the deities would be angry with me! I would request them to adjust the previous day's account appropriately!

I would have camphor pieces in my trouser pocket carefully folded in pieces of paper, with the name of the temple and deity written on each paper. Camphor pills were expensive, so I used to buy camphor chunks and cut it into small pieces. In cutting, I was very careful to cut them equally, lest there was partial division. If by mistake a piece became big, that piece would go to

Annamalayar – the main deity in the temple of Arunachala. For Annamalayar I had no problem in giving the big piece. There was no scope for comparison where he was concerned!

If I missed lighting the camphor pieces, I would light two quotas on my way back at each temple, to make up for the loss. On those days, it would take that much longer to reach home! There was an order of temples… First it was Karpaga Vinayagar Temple, then the Police Station Mariyamman Temple, then Annamalayar temple, then Vallabha Vinayagar temple, then the temple in front of Sri V. Thaanmal Sowkar Jain Higher Secondary School, then I would enter into the school, that's all!

My brother used to feel very bored and would keep cursing me when he was waiting outside every temple. And I would not just bow down to the main deity and come away; I would bow down to the Dwarabalakars (the two deities that man the entrance to the main deity as guards), enquire after them and their health, offer worship to the Nandi (the bull that adorns the temple entrance) and so on!

My brother would pedal fast whenever a temple approached, hoping I would miss seeing it, but I never missed it! I would scream out, 'Hey! The Vinayagar temple has come, stop! Stop!' And he would stop. On the days his patience got rough, I would walk to school instead of getting a ride, but after two to three days, he would feel sad for me and offer to take me by bicycle once again!

At least my younger brother was inclined towards temples and worship. My older brother was not very inclined and he used to curse me after kicking in the stand of his cycle to wait for me outside each temple. Sometimes, I would start reciting the appropriate mantras much ahead of reaching the temple, afraid that he would scold me for taking long. When the cycle took the turn to the temple, I would start reciting. So I would finish by the time we reached the temple. Then I would tell him that I would just do the circumambulation, light the camphor and come out.

I never learnt cycling before the age of 12. And after my first experience at the age of 12, I couldn't ride a bicycle anymore. (At this point in time, one of the disciples commented, 'Swamiji, even at that time in Tiruvannamalai, you had a driver!' to which He laughed and concurred.) I never knew that my inability to ride a bicycle was because of my spiritual experience. I was not aware that it had to do with decreased body consciousness that happened after that experience. I used to think I did not have the ability to ride a cycle, that's all. I was also never aware that there was something great in me. I used to think that everyone was like me. I simply took it for granted. Only later on I realized that it is not for all.

nithyananda took to meditating in the cremation grounds in the outskirts of Tiruvannamalai. Extended hours, through the night, absorbed in the vibrant silence of Arunachala, he would sit in meditation, ardently feeling the intimacy with Arunachala, deeply yearning to become one with it. At the break of dawn, he would return home. Completely convinced that they were only guardians of their second son, his parents totally accepted nithyananda's strange routines as pure *lila* (divine play) of Existence.

Chapter - 7

Leaving Home

Why an Ashram environment is needed for spiritual growth?

nithyananda's family was a large joint family in Tiruvannamalai. There were well over 20 families who lived together in a large house that was almost two acres (nearly 90,000 square feet) in built up area.

Nithyananda says:

'People ask me now why I have ashrams. What is the point in living in ashrams, as if in a commune? What difference is it from living in a joint family?'

We need to think of humans as conscious beings and not as a social utility. If you are a doctor, your profession is a doctor; your being is not a doctor. The Master is trying to help you reclaim your inner space, your being. You are more than a doctor; you are your inner space. In his ashram, Nithyananda is helping people to gain their inner space. In comparison to this inner space, the outer space that we have spent all our time in, will seem so small and insignificant. One will no longer care for it. We will not care whether we have it or not.

Outer life is only one part of our life. You may ask, 'Why can't I reach this state from my own home? Why is the ashram necessary?'

Your home is based on the concept of society. It makes you forget the truth. The ideology of the inner space is the backbone of the ashram; its ambience, its structure, everything in it beholds this ideology. Your friends and your Master will not let you forget this. For 10 days after meeting the Master, after hearing His discourse, His meditation course, we will be in a high mood at home.

Then society takes over us; the bondage returns. People who interact with us make a difference. Body language is the food for the mind. It is important that the very body language of the people we move with keeps us in the right current. In the ashram, the food is positive. People who we are with, help us overcome our weaknesses instead of exploiting them. They do not judge or criticize. Society on the other hand constantly judges us; if we conform, we are rewarded; if we do not, we are punished.

The ashram is a higher reality. Buddha talked about following *buddha* (the Master himself), *sanga* (the community created by the Master) and *dhamma* (the Master's teachings) in order to reach the Ultimate Truth of Existence. The *sanga*, which is what is implied by the ashram life, provides the environment for the path to wisdom. Even if we do not remember our path, *sanga,* the community, the ashram, will remind us. Someone around us will constantly remind us of the higher ideals we have set out to reach. We would have a loving and caring place to grow spiritually. In the outer world, people will disturb, obstruct and stop us from our spiritual path bringing in their intellect and limited perceptions. In the ashram, people encourage us in reaching out to the great Truths.

Human beings cannot live as isolated structures, as just individuals. *No man is an island*, John Donne has said. The human being is a social animal. If we are constantly reminded of higher Truths, we shall live them, radiate them. *Sanga* is about having bliss, radiating bliss. That's why ashrams are created.

Ashrams are epicenters of strong blissful vibrations; vibrations that cause the inner space to quake and shift; whatever we had built before is shattered and leveled.

When one sits at the feet of the Master, all doubts are removed; energy is created to fulfill desires to reach higher spiritual levels. It is easy to love the Master; it is much harder to love our fellow beings. In the ashram, people learn to love each other without conditions and causes. Bliss is shared independent of the Master.

The ashram is an ideological joint family. It is not bondage of blood relationship. It is a deep emotional and ideological connection. Ashram life is a way of life and one needs maturity. It is not a theory but a reality to be expressed and experienced.

One does not have to renounce worldly and material life to be part of the ashram community. In Nithyananda ashrams around the world, couples and families live together in harmony, following a common dream while at the same time pursuing their material vocation. It is a joint family, not related by blood, but by conviction and the radial linkage to the Master. It is a bond that is much stronger than any blood relationship.

The ashram life does require maturity to be a part of it. One has to be in a relatively ego less state to coexist with others in a mode of true equality. It is an environment where each one compensates for another's weakness and shares one's strength with another. There is no compulsion for anyone to do what he or she is told. Some may do all the work. Some may do nothing. Tolerance for another being, understanding of another being and acceptance of another being lead to compassion for one another. This leads to the understanding that 'the whole world is my family', *Vasudeva Kutumbaha* (The family of Lord Krishna), as Lord Krishna had said.

Vivekananda said, 'the *dharma chakra* (the wheel of righteousness) is in motion. All you have to do is to stand by it and be part of its motion.' The ashram environment allows you to be a part of the moving *chakra* perpetually.

Distaste for Society's hypocrisy

A paternal Grandmother of nithyananda was about 104 when she died, and nithyananda was about 12 then. This lady, whose name was Kannamma, had no children of her own and was looked after by one of nithyananda's uncles. The uncle and his wife were not happy looking after this lady, and always found some excuse or another not to be of help to her. The lady herself was a difficult and unpleasant person. She was very miserly even though she was wealthy. She often would ask nithyananda to buy her tobacco, and when the boy asked for money, she would tell him to ask his father. This old lady would even grudge giving water from the common well inside the house to her neighbors when there was a drought.

When she died, no one in the family wept! The most caring person was the neighborhood doctor who attended to her, who had been treated shabbily by her and who had even been refused water by her in the past. Yet, with great compassion he treated her until her death.

Just before the family expected mourners to arrive, the women in the household changed into cheap *saris* and removed all their jewelry. As soon as the guests arrived, they started wailing as if on cue. Once the formal wailing ceremony was over as a mere ritual, they would get into inane social conversation, offer refreshments and coffee to guest mourners. Every time a new set of relatives arrived, the wailing cycle would start all over again. nithyananda was shocked and surprised at the hypocrisy of it all.

While the dead body was still in the house and relatives were still calling upon the family to condole, the immediate family went into the dead lady's private room, where her box of jewelry was kept under her bed. There were 27 families living under one roof; they all laid claim to her jewelry and other possessions and started negotiating and bargaining even before her body got cold. The family called the goldsmith to assay and value the jewelry.

In that moment, nithyananda lost all respect for his family and its social conditioning. He started laughing loudly at their behavior. An uncle tried to hit him to stop his laughter, as he thought that the boy was getting hysterical out of emotional shock. nithyananda held his uncle's hand and told him that if he tried to hit him again he would tell all the assembled crowd what the family members were up to; bargaining about sharing the loot even before the body was cremated. nithyananda's mother told the uncle to be careful of her son, as he was quite capable of doing what he threatened to do. She tried to persuade him to eat to divert him. The relatives then haggled about who would pay for the funeral expenses. nithyananda's father, a mild and innocent man, who hated arguments, immediately agreed to take care of all expenses to avoid any dispute on this score.

Completely disgusted, nithyananda took his book of the Bhagavad Gita and started chanting the verses in front of the dead body. (By then, he had had first spiritual experience). That was probably the only action that helped the old lady's spirit depart peacefully amidst all the drama that was going on. Nithyananda later told us: *That was the first conscious death that happened in my Presence.*

Moving away from home

nithyananda always, from early childhood, had the dream of becoming a *sanyasi*, an ascetic mendicant. In his family, boys and girls who were still in their early teens, were matched for future marriage. This was done as soon as the girls reached adolescence. A suitable match was selected within the family network. Very rarely was there any opposition to these arranged matches. Both girl and boy were constantly reminded of their relationship and as far as the family was concerned it was all a done thing; and so it was with the boy and the girl; they never considered any alternatives.

nithyananda's elder brother had already been matched with a relative when he was about 14 and it was nithyananda's turn now. With great fervor, the family started discussing possibilities. One day, an elderly relative, a lady, started discussing this in front of nithyananda. The boy stared hard at her. The lady became uncomfortable and asked him why he was staring at her. nithyananda continued to stare and looked hard into her eyes. She understood that he did not like her discussing his marriage and asked what he had against marriage and why he was upset. nithyananda asked her rather rudely, and unusually for him, 'What have you achieved by marrying?' The lady did not reply; instead she asked him what he wanted to be when he grew up. nithyananda promptly and without a trace of doubt replied that he wanted to be - a *swami*, a *sanyasi*. He drew a picture of how he would look when he grew up. The picture was that of a Hindu monk with a turban, the headdress Nithyananda sports today.

nithyananda's mother had understood her son's inclinations to become an ascetic. nithyananda was very close to his mother. Even when he was in his mid teens, he used to lie down with his head on her lap and talk to her about his spiritual experiences. He used to spend a lot of time in the kitchen talking to his mother. On occasions when nithyananda used to laugh, joke and play the fool, he would find his mother suddenly turn sad with tears in her eyes. It was as if she knew for certain that he would leave her and go away soon.

In Indian families, especially in such small towns, in joint families as with nithyananda's, the sons continued to stay with the parents even after marriage; under parental control and under the same roof.

Sons inherited the family wealth and needed to be part of the family; daughters on the other hand, became part of their husbands' families once they were married.

Nithyananda had been having the urge to leave home as a *sanyasi* since his early teens. By this time, he was seventeen and had completed his diploma in Mechanical Engineering in Gudiyattam nearby Tiruvannamalai.

Academics was purely incidental in nithyananda's pursuit of the Truth. He spent hardly any time with his books. With just the total concentration that he gave during the class hours, he saw his exams through with a distinction. After finishing his high school in Tiruvannamalai, nithyananda went to study Mechanical Engineering at a Polytechnic Institute in nearby Gudiyattam. He stayed at a lodge in the town. Even during this period when he was away from home, nithyananda spent his time alone in meditation, unlike his friends who used to spend time having fun and watching movies. Here too, he rarely spent time studying and yet fared very well in his exams.

When one of his friends asked him what he was going to achieve in such long wasteful hours of meditation, nithyananda replied, 'One day, you will stand in line to receive my blessings. Then you will know.'

During a recent tour of Tamilnadu, in his hometown of Tiruvannamalai, the Master beckoned us near him onto the stage of a packed hall and pointed to his friends, waiting in queue to take his blessings after he had delivered a discourse and meditation. The boys could be seen choked with emotion, and shaking uncontrollably, as they bowed down to touch the feet of the Master. We looked on, caught in our own emotions, as he took them in his arms with mischievous laughter and ardent compassion.

The urge to leave home after completion of his diploma became unmanageable. He felt he was ready to leave. He felt that he could not continue living the way he was at home. His whole life seemed a lie. It was suffocating to live under social bondage.

Recently we stumbled upon some archival material at the Bidadi ashram and came across a few pages from a diary written by nithyananda in Tamil when he was seventeen. These writings indicated what triggered his departure from home.

On 15 July 1994 nithyananda wrote:

I took all the papers and talisman given by K.S. Narayanaswami Thatha, read the papers, tore them up, and threw everything in the well and in the garbage pile.

On 16 July 1994 he wrote:

Today is the great day when Brahmasukhi was kicked by a man and received correctional wisdom just the same way as the Saint Pattinatthar received enlightenment from the blows of a woman! After an hour and a half of deep meditation, mind became fully focused.

*The title given to him by Kuppammal in her letter of initiation

On 17 July 1994, he wrote:

Today I meditated for half hour to one hour. Mind was at peace. No rapprochement with him. He is angry. Even when I spoke he does not respond properly.

On 18 July 1994, he wrote finally:

Let my mind win over my senses! Since my wisdom has not matured the same way as my mind has, it behaves in its own way. To enhance my wisdom, it is good to do *pranayama* (controlled breathing meditation) daily from 11 pm till 1 am.

This sequence of incidents referred to a meeting that nithyananda had with a *Siddhar*, a mystic who had great wisdom and one who had achieved great powers. nithyananda had started spending time with these traveling, wandering mystics in Tiruvannamalai, much in the same way as Ramakrishna *Paramahamsa* did and learnt many spiritual techniques from them.

He used to regularly meet with this *Siddhar*, an eighty-year-old man, who used to sit in a small *mandap* (an open shelter) in the *Girivala* (the path around the Arunachala Hill). The *Siddhar* was like a mad man and everyone used to refer to him only in first person. He had a bowl in front of him and people used to drop food into it. He used to eat and leave the bowl unwashed. Stray dogs would come and lick it up. Passersby would again drop food in the same bowl and he used to eat that as well. If someone washed the bowl, the bowl got clean else it would remain that way.

That was also the time, nithyananda had internalized a number of *tantric* techniques taught to him by Narayanaswami Thatha (about whom we read earlier) and using these powers started predicting events and materializing objects for his friends. He indulged a lot in energy play for the fun of it, with only positive connotations though. This *Siddhar* however, told nithyananda one day, that his ardent indulgence in energy play was like prostituting himself and that he should give up all these practices which are actually stalling his pure spiritual growth. He compared nithyananda to Pattinatthar, a famous Tamil personality, who lusted after women despite his spiritual inclinations.

Nithyananda, when he was showing us the pieces of paper with the above written on them, recalled these sequence of events. He said that on that day when the *Siddhar* admonished him and kicked him, he threw away all the *mantra* he had written down and the talismans given by Narayanaswami Thatha, and dedicated himself to meditation.

When describing this milestone event in his life that triggered his departure from home, Nithyananda said to us:

'Like how boys of my age were caught in lust and gave into it, I was caught in energy play and indulged in it heartily. When the *Siddhar* told me that I was prostituting myself like Pattinathar, I tore the *thaayathu* (talisman) given by Narayanaswami Thatha, although I did not tell him that I tore it. The next day, he beat me up. The blow that he gave had a far greater psychological effect than physical effect. It was like a cognitive shift. Like how the moment Pattinathar understood the saying *kaadatra oosiyum vaaraathu kaan kadai vazhikkae* (a needle without a ear, a hole, is of no earthly use), he dropped all his habits, renounced all his wealth and went away to Varanasi (a holy town in North India), the blow that the mystic gave me was like a lightning stroke that awakened me. I left all power play and left home soon as well.

If you read these bits of papers, you can clearly see the play of the mind before the final decision was taken. Just look at the thought trend in just those few days' time. For those few days that the encounter with the mystic was happening, my mind was swaying like a pendulum. At one point in time, I tore the talisman given by Thatha; the next moment, I contemplated bringing the torn talisman back, thinking I might have done wrong in tearing it. The mind was so disturbed that I advocated myself to do *pranayama* to control it and attain to peace! I have even recorded at that time, that on one occasion, the mystic did not talk to me properly and my mind was more disturbed because of this. To me, those wandering mystics were my soul mates and I could not bear it when they did not respond to me properly. I have recorded clearly that I understood that the turmoil was because my wisdom had not matured as my mind had; that my intellect was fine but it had not become an experience and so the practices and the confusion; that *pranayama* will help in settling down. But finally, the shift happened within and the decision never again to indulge in energy play was taken! Look how closely I was watching my mind at that age! That incident and those few days were like a process, a technique for me.

I underwent turmoil before giving up. Just these 4 bits of paper are like a process, like a technique for anyone who reads it as well, if one relates to the sequence with keen awareness. These pieces of paper show that the meditation, the penance *itself* happened with understanding and that the understanding did not come only as a result of enlightenment.

You need to understand one thing: There was no one in my life to tell me: 'do this', 'do that', 'if you do this, you will attain' etc. And, there was no living proof either to show me that if I did all those things, I will attain. There was no living Master to show me through his own experiences of attaining. Despite this, I moved on, with great faith in Existence, drawing intelligence from the Cosmic source.'

Soon after this incident, nithyananda felt it was time to leave home. Suddenly one evening, the urge was so strong that he decided he needed to act immediately. He felt he had to jump out of the life he was leading and into the life he was seeking without further delay. He could not bear to continue living the way he did any longer.

nithyananda had to tell his mother first. He loved her deeply and wanted to make sure that her shock and suffering was as little as possible. That night, when the urge was so strong that he felt he must depart, nithyananda went to his mother around 10 pm in the night. He asked her, 'What would you do if I died?' His mother asked, 'Why do you ask such an inauspicious question? What is wrong?'

nithyananda said, 'Nothing, no particular reason, I just need to know.' His mother said resignedly, 'What will I do? I need to accept it if it happens.'

nithyananda then told her that he wanted to leave home.

His mother burst into tears. Her body shook in sorrow uncontrollably. 'I knew that you would go away one day,' she said. nithyananda asked her whether she did not want him to leave.

She said, 'No, I know that you want to go and I want you to do what you have always wanted to do in your life. I cannot stop you from that; but I cannot bear to see you go. That is why I am crying.'

nithyananda felt overwhelmed at this unconditional love of his mother. She was in deep sorrow and yet she wanted for her son what *he* wanted. She did not wish to be in his way. Her innocence and selfless love touched him deeply. She was innocent of her own innocence.

nithyananda had not expected his mother to accept the reality of her losing him so easily. It was as if there was a divine hand in this. When one is intensely in tune with the divine, things fall in place and all obstructions disappear. When nithyananda's father returned home from his work, his mother told him what her son had told her earlier that night. nithyananda's father was angry with her. He felt that she had done something to annoy their son, which caused him to want to move away from home. nithyananda told his father that there was nothing his mother or any one else in the family had done or said that led to his decision to leave home. He told his father that he had always wanted to lead the life of a *sanyasi* and he felt that this was the time for him to leave home in that pursuit.

nithyananda was fortunate that his parents were not sophisticated and corrupted by societal influences. They were naïve and innocent in many ways. All that they really wanted was that their son did what made him happy. They knew from the time of his birth when the family astrologer had predicted that he would be a *raja sanyasi,* that he would leave home sooner or later. Their hope was that it would be later. They were concerned about how he would take care of himself, and where he would find shelter and where he would find food, since nithyananda had rarely ventured out of Tiruvannamalai.

Nithyananda is worshipped today by millions. Back in 1995, when he was ready to leave home, no one knew who he was. nithyananda himself had no idea then what would happen to him.

He knew that he wanted to be enlightened, and he thought it would happen sometime before he died, perhaps when he was 70 or 80. He had no clue as to what Existence had in store for him, nor did he know then that he was to surrender to Existence every step of the way. He told a group of us one day, 'My idea at that time was, I would get enlightened through intense perseverance and meditation and after attaining, be by myself in my enlightened state. Little did I know that Existence had planned a grand mission!

nithyananda told his parents that he wanted to leave in a week's time. Back then he was clear that he would not come back to the South at all. His heart was set on spending his time in the Himalayan mountains. His father, though he did not say much and did not try to stop his son, made his displeasure and unhappiness felt by his attitude towards nithyananda's mother.

nithyananda was sorry for his mother and tried to convince his father without much success, that the decision to leave had nothing to do with his relationship with the family, and that it sprang from a desire deep within him. nithyananda's mother was being buffeted between father and son; her husband felt that she was responsible for their son leaving home. She was heartbroken at her son leaving home. Both parents did not know when they would see their son again or whether they would see him alive again at all.

Years later, when we were on a trip to the Himalayas with our dear Master, his parents were with us as well and a few of us in the bus had the wonderful opportunity to hear him talk to them about the particular time he decided to leave home! He recalled the events that happened at that time and asked them for the first time how they felt when he was leaving home! We listened avidly. His mother told him that they knew from his birth that he would leave them one day. They were happy that he would become a great *sanyasi* as predicted by the astrologer; but that they were not able to bear the parting. She also said that they had to bear the brunt of social repercussions but they sailed through it with not much difficulty.

When Nithyananda returned to Tiruvannamalai for the first time after His enlightenment, as soon as He stepped into the town area, He tripped on a stone. When he looked down, He found that it was a *Siva linga* that seemed to have positioned itself there to welcome Him home. From childhood, His grandfather had repeatedly told nithyananda that Arunachaleswar and Unnamalai Amman were his parents, and nithyananda had always considered Arunachala to be his home.

Nithyananda took the *Siva lingam* in His hands and went to see His mother to get her blessings. Later on, one of the Brahmachari at the ashram asked Nithyananda how it was possible for Him to seek the blessings of another person, even if it was His mother, after enlightenment. Once enlightened, the Master has to bless others, not take their blessings.

Nithyananda explained:

'By the time I was enlightened, as a result of my meditation and penance most of my samskara and past experiences had dissolved. However, I found some traces, some blocks still remained. I searched within and found it was a feeling of guilt. When I left home and had asked my mother for permission to leave, she just shed tears and said that there was nothing for her to say and it was my own decision. She added that you have decided to become a *sanyasi*, but I cannot bear it and I am crying because I cannot bear it; don't be troubled.'

The words of his mother, helpless and not expecting any response, remained in nithyananda's inner self as an energy block of guilt. When he looked at this with awareness that too dissolved and he was immersed in bliss and was enlightened.

Nithyananda said that it was to express gratitude for this incident that He wanted to seek His mother's blessings.

nithyananda's mother was also his first disciple. Whenever there was an issue that confused her, she sought him out for counsel. Whenever she thought something was important, including what television to buy, nithyananda was the one she would turn to. Even then both his parents used to call him, *swami*!

Many a time, I have sat with this wonderful lady and talked to her about things in general and our Master in particular. Nithyananda's father died in November 2005 and His mother now lives in Bidadi in the ashram. She attends all the regular puja done in the ashram, but no one knows that she is Nithyananda's mother; such is her simplicity and detachment. She says openly that she hardly understands anything of the philosophical truths that Nithyananda talks about, and that she is just content to sit and listen. Nithyananda recently ordained her as a sanyasi. When her turn came to take up the saffron clothes, He laughingly asked her as He did everyone else, 'have you asked your parents for permissions?' since her parents are still alive.
She answered simply, 'No Swami, I just left home and came to you.'

Time and again Nithyananda talks about the innocence, simplicity and total lack of guile of both His parents and how much that helped Him to continue on His path with no obstacles.

News spread amongst the close-knit family circle of nithyananda that he was leaving home. Friends and relatives gathered as if to condole, and the house had become a place of mourning. nithyananda used to sit in a sofa in the center of the house and all visitors would sit around him looking at him sadly and crying. They all knew that he would certainly leave and yet some would try and persuade him not to. The answers that nithyananda gave them were curt and honest and very different from his normally very polite behavior. This stopped them from asking more questions.

An uncle questioned nithyananda as to why he was leaving and asked, 'Are we all not spiritual people?' nithyananda shot back saying, 'You drink from morning till evening. What do you know about spirituality?' The uncle shut up and left the house insulted. It was unusual for a boy to leave home at seventeen or a girl to leave home till marriage in rural India. In many joint families, the sons continue to live with their parents till the father dies and one of them takes over the family responsibilities.

nithyananda warned his mother that all the family wealth will disappear once he left home. He told her not to be concerned as there would always be enough for her and his father to live comfortably though not lavishly. His mother was not bothered about the wealth issue; she was only worried about who would feed her son as he wandered in wilderness.

Nithyananda said of His parents, once when discussing prarabda karma and how the spirit chooses a body of suitable environment. 'My parents had tremendous innocence. They were so innocent that they were not even aware of their innocence. They never interfered in anything I did. They never disturbed me. Whenever I brought school report cards for him to sign, he will say you sign and take it back! They never protected me either; not from pain and accidents. They let me be. They let me grow with intelligence and visualization.'

When he left home, nithyananda said to his mother, 'Whoever takes care of everything, will take care of you. She will take care of all your basic needs. Your last days will be with me.'

Later Nithyananda came to know that these very words were used when Ramakrishna *Paramahamsa* blessed the family of Vivekananda, when Ramakrishna gave Vivekananda sanyas, 'Whoever takes care of everything will take care of you!'

We were together, Master, His mother and I, when He recounted this incident with a huge smile on His face. I turned to look at His mother, as if for confirmation. All she could do was to nod silently, with tears in her eyes. She just said, 'You are there Swami; that's enough. I am blessed.'

nithyananda's mother's family was quite spiritually inclined, though his father's family was quite the opposite. nithyananda's maternal grandfather was nithyananda's first inspiration, who carried him on his shoulder, told him stories, and created the first positive *samskara* (desires) in the young boy. His grandfather told him time and again that he should be like a Prahlad, Dhruv or Markandeya, all Masters who were enlightened before adolescence. One wonders whether he knew what was in store for the young child, who as he desired did have his first spiritual experience when he was still pre-adolescent.

Some of the relatives suggested that nithyananda stay in a local religious institution that trained monks so that they would know he was safe and could keep an eye on him. His grandfather said that he would build an ashram for him so that he need not go anywhere to pursue his spiritual quest, as there was no greater spiritual center than Tiruvannamalai. nithyananda laughed and told him that they would only let him stay there for two days; they would then ask him to come back home once a week, then twice a week and finally he might as well stay home, get a job and get married. His grandfather said, 'no, no, no one will disturb you.' nithyananda had no patience to listen to all this.

Someone then said, 'Let us get him married within two or three days; let us select a girl.' They started discussing what dowry to ask for! It was all a matter of family prestige. 'How can we let him do this? What will people say when they hear that a son has walked out of the family?' Lots of discussions went on. Some people wanted nithyananda guarded so that he could not run away.

An uncle from Chennai (known as Madras earlier), his mother's brother, suggested that nithyananda stay with him in Chennai for a while before he decided to leave. nithyananda thought that was a good idea. Intuitively, nithyananda felt that this would help. He wanted to go north to the Himalaya. He knew that he had to start from Chennai by train to reach the Himalaya. It was also a blessing, since he had already decided that he would not touch any money once he started his wandering. In a train in India it is still possible to travel without a ticket whereas in a bus it is impossible, and to reach Chennai he had to travel by bus, for which he would have no money. Things were indeed falling into place!

Before he left Tiruvannamalai, nithyananda went to the temple of Arunachala, and stood at the sanctum sanctorum in front of Arunachaleshwara. For the first time, he felt the extent of the depth of his connection to Arunachaleshwara. He did not feel he was going to miss Him. No; but he was sad he was going to miss all His festivities and functions. As he stood in front of his beloved Arunachaleshwara, tears flowed unceasingly from his eyes. nithyananda could see the living energy behind the idol radiating compassion and blessing. He heard a distinct voice, the Lord blessing him, 'You will come back to me, you will come back successfully.' nithyananda prostrated before the idol and took leave with deep love and fulfillment. nithyananda felt that Arunachaleshwara was with him in this journey.

Whenever nithyananda traveled by bus from Tiruvannamalai, he would keep looking back till the mountain Arunachala was out of his sight. This would normally take about half an hour after the trip started. This time as he traveled to Chennai, the boy continued to see the mountain till he suddenly woke up when the bus reached Chennai and he realized that he had slept through the trip dreaming of his beloved Arunachala. His inner space was filled with the grace of Arunachala.

In fact, the only problem that nithyananda had in leaving his home was in leaving Arunachala. After his experience with Arunagiri Yogiswara, this was the only time in his life that he felt that he would be missing something. Whenever people had talked to him about the fact that he would miss one thing or another when he left home, it did not make any sense to him. It was only when he came to bid farewell to his dear Arunachaleshwara at the temple that he did for the first time feel that he was about to lose something.

He never thought he would ever return. His goal was enlightenment, which he thought would happen when he was old, eighty or ninety, before he died.

When he stood at the *garba graham*, the inner sanctum of the temple, the form of the idol filled his mind. Whatever one sees normally is stored in the eyes; whatever one sees intensely is stored in the mind. Anything that is stored this way inside, in the mind, will attract one's attention again and again. The moment he strongly felt that he would not see the idol again, it was as if the form of the idol left him. The feeling of missing disappeared.

Fish see the Swan's reflection and wish to own it

Soon after his enlightenment, Nithyananda had a vision of the mission that he had been sent out to accomplish. He perceived this mission as an endeavor to transform people, their attitudes and mindsets through meditation, towards the path of realizing that people are divine in nature. There was a strong impulse for him to go back to the South of India where he came from, even though he had determined when he left home that he would not return.

Along with these messages that came to him, Nithyananda 'downloaded the vision of a Swan' soon after his enlightenment. That Swan, the *Paramahamsa*, is now the emblem of Dhyanapeetam, the spiritual center of Nithyananda's mission. Dhyanapeetam was established and later extended to the Nithyananda Foundation to teach people how to transform.

In later days when Nithyananda reflected upon the vision of this great Swan called the *Paramahamsa*, he had these insights to offer us. The metaphor of the Swan was Nithyananda himself and the fish that see the Swan, his disciples:

A great Swan, the *Paramahamsa* is flying high in the sky. Its reflection is seen on a series of ponds far below on the earth. The fish in the ponds see this reflection of the Swan and rejoice. The very sight of the reflection fills them with joy. Schools of fish start marking off areas which they claim are their own within which they want to capture the Swan's reflection. They build fences and compound walls to contain the reflection. Some fish build temples for the Swan. Some fish build ashrams. The fish hope to contain the Swan within these boundaries believing that the reflection will remain under their possession.

The Swan neither knows what is going on below upon the land, nor is it bothered about the drama of the fish. It continues to fly. It never lands.

It's the shadow, the reflection that the fish perceive as moving. The fish too move. The water too is moving. The fish cannot distinguish between the reflection and the source.

The fish are very excited about the Swan in the water. Some fish feel they are getting enlightened. They feel that the closer they are to the reflection, the faster they will get enlightened!

If only the fish would raise their eyes, they would see the real Swan, the source of the reflection that they are chasing. However, the reflection itself is so graceful, so beautiful, that most fish have no motivation to look up. The fish are quite happy building walls and fences in the water, with the belief that they are able to hold the Swan and possess its reflection.

If they do look up and see beyond the reflection, they too will become the Swan; then they will be really enlightened.

The reflection comes and goes even as the Swan flies past the ponds and returns; in many forms: Jesus, Krishna, Buddha and others; different angles, different perspectives, and different distortions. If the water is calm, the fish see one reflection; if water is turbulent they see another; when they move with the water they see yet another form. They argue with each other, claiming that what each one sees is the real Swan; all by looking at the reflection. Each one's reflection is possessed by that individual fish or groups of fish, not to be shared.

They don't even wait till the reflection goes beyond the limits of the pond before arguing about the reality of the Swan as they see it. The Swan just keeps flying, the fish just keep arguing. The fish miss the present, miss the reality in the whole game.

Are the fish also part of the reflection? The illusion of what is going on?

When they do not see the swan's reflection, the fish have no recollection of the reflection that had filled them with joy just a while ago. Their memories are short and they are back to their eating, mating, fighting and dying!

It is only when they see the reflection, and with it the joy it brings, that their spiritual drama begins again. If they do not see the reflection, there will be no Swan, no movement. The water does not hold imprints of the Swan. The water does not move with the Swan. The Swan does not know about its reflection. Only the fish react. They react when they see the reflection.

Some fish make a website for the swan. Others bring out books on it. As the Swan's reflection crosses the pond, different groups say, 'We in Seattle own the Swan; we in Vancouver own the Swan; the Swan belongs to Bangalore, etc.' Yet very few fish look up. They are all so focused on and obsessed with the reflection.

Zen Koans, Buddhist Sutras, Sufi Stories, Christian Parables, Hindu mantras - all say the same thing: Look up! Look within!

When the fish come close to the reflection, the form gets distorted. They cannot see clearly any more. The fish need to look up, look within.

When Truth is expressed, the facts become meaningless. The vision of the reflection by the fish is factual; the vision of the Swan is the Truth.

When one perceives with the intellect, one is still far from Truth. One should get closer and feel with the heart. When one gets closer, one experiences through the senses. When one gets really close, eyes no longer see clearly. What can be seen is only through the being. What is seen through the being is the Truth; that is the witnessing consciousness.

When the witnessing consciousness is at work, what is right for you will happen. Every thought that arises in you will be fulfilled. What you see will be the Source, not the reflection. That is the level at which enlightened Masters operate.

Siddha, spiritual technology practitioners and mystics who are not enlightened, can also make their desires come true through visualization and such other techniques; however, they do not do it in conscious awareness, and can get into serious trouble by operating through their unconscious.

Some fish will write all this down as well! That will not be the Truth. Truth is multidimensional. Any writing, however good, will only be two-dimensional. But of course, it needs to be written to offer inspiration to seekers to experience the Swan in them.

When nithyananda left home after his first spiritual experience, he had a clear understanding of how ephemeral social life was. However, his mind was not empty. It still had an alloying element that separated the near enlightened fish from the Swan. The wanderings and the penance burnt out the remnants of the alloy; the mind was left behind purposely so that the final union could take place. Finally the fish looked up and became the Swan; nithyananda became Nithyananda.

In turn, the Swan awaits other fish to look up so that they too can join him in the sky!

Mystery, Thou art My Master

'It is a riddle wrapped in a mystery inside an enigma,' said Churchill famously of Russia during World War II.

Without any reservation we could use this expression for our Master. Or perhaps we could even go further: He is a puzzle in a riddle wrapped in a mystery inside an enigma!

I remember the time when the Master was elaborating upon the Siva Sutra to us. Siva Sutras is an ancient Hindu scripture in which Lord Siva, the Rejuvenator answers questions posed by Devi, His consort. This day was the fifth day of the Siva Sutra lectures.

Devi asks Siva, 'What is life, beyond form, pervading forms?'

We sit in front of him as in the days of the *Upanishad,* disciples at the feet of the Master.

There is no order; no chaos. There is neither respect nor insolence. Men do not sit on one side; or women on the other. There is no chatter; but no silence either. There are no questions; mere doubts. There is no desperation; just acceptance. There are electronic gadgets on one side; ritual implements on the other. No greed is evident; nor guilt. No anger visible; nor helplessness. The assembly is a motley mix of genders, ages, professions and interests; all with one purpose- to hear the Master expound upon the timeless Truths.

The Master sits with a smile, inscrutable as the Sphinx.
Who is he? Is he the Father, Mother, Son, Brother, Friend, Lover or a Fake? We know he would love to be called a Fake; that would make the confusion more complete. Is he all forms in one? He can be the terror of Siva; he can also be the nectar of Krishna. Is he better as a bitter nightmare or a sweet fantasy?

There are times when he chides, eyes aglow with anger. One learns to stay quiet with acceptance. The grimace morphs into a grin; Siva morphs into Krishna. Tears come to my eyes even as I write; and as I read what I write; what to speak of being in his presence.

He is all forms; and no form. He refuses to be captured in a frame, turned into a stone, worshipped as an image; he would then be a Master dying at the hands of the fantasies of his devotees. He would rather be the '*simha swapna*', the nightmare, awakening us into wisdom; to be the Zen stick that prods us into wakefulness, than to be the crutch that we are comfortable with. He relates to us on multiple frames and planes, just to keep us off balance and in confusion, than allow to be frozen into one frame that kills the Master and ourselves.

The Master is beyond forms; beyond dimensions. He is not uni, bi, tri or multi dimensioned. His dimensions and forms are infinity; infinite dimensional; infiniD, so to say.

He said to us:

To each one of you I am different. The way I interact with one person depends on the needs of the being of that person, which even that person may not understand. Do not discuss with one another how I treat you and work with you individually and personally. You will only cause misunderstanding and confusion. Do not try and put me in a frame. 'Oh, you are Krishna, you are Siva, you are Mother etc'. I will not allow myself to be put in a frame. The moment you box me in a frame, I die. I am a living Master. I change every instant. Do not try to predict my actions, my words, my thoughts; you will only have suffering.
Frozen into one frame, Mother or Lover, I am easy for you to capture and retain. I am then easier to market. It's good business for me, not good business for you. I want you to be confused so that you become enlightened. I want you to die so that you are reborn. Come to me with your ignorance; it's my duty to show you the path. Don't hesitate to fall into my arms with love; you will soar with me into bliss.

We are so used to falling into mud that we hesitate. Soaring into bliss is not our nature as we understand it. Our anxieties and fears work upon us creating nightmares and fantasies.

There was a far deeper meaning in what the Master said than was obvious. He wanted each one to flow with him as he was at every moment; savor him here and now. People worry about when they will see him next while they are still in his presence. He says, 'what foolishness! Just enjoy my presence. By thinking about when you will see me next, you are wasting the opportunity to be joyful now. Grab this moment. Just be.'

It is not for the disciple to unravel the mystery of his Master; not even to try and understand; the proposition is doomed to be a failure. All one can do is to BE, and to enjoy the bliss of that moment.

He said these words in the Himalayan trip with him in the year 2005, while talking about the relationship with the Master:

Who is the Master, the Guru? The Guru is a being in whom Nithya Ananda or Eternal Bliss is expressed; one who creates and transmits a formula and the space for others to experience the same eternally - without the need for the formula and space. From time immemorial, the Guru-sishya parampara (Master-disciple relationship) started in the Himalayas. It is the oldest of relationships. The very idea of relating with one another started only after this relationship.
It is also the last relationship before enlightenment. Before this, humans were like animals, barbaric, in whatever culture and religion. All civilizations started with the advent of the Master-disciple relationship. Even Masters who taught that there was no need for a Guru, like J Krishnamurthy, became Gurus despite themselves. All knowledge, not just spiritual, needs a Guru, the person who leads us from darkness to light, from ignorance to knowledge.

In modern days, people tend to question the need for a spiritual Guru, but not the other kinds. People respect those who teach a skill that helps them earn money, but spiritual Masters come by as optional. Spirituality is not an option, something esoteric, something magical, something unattainable. It is the state in which we are in mentally and physically - sound and happy, our relationships with one another are productive and fruitful, and in addition we have the awareness of what we are doing at every instant. This awareness makes us spontaneous, grounds us in the present, and makes us truly responsible for our thoughts, words and actions. Each individual needs to attain this state for one's own good as well as that of others around.

If you understand this truth and respect spiritual knowledge, you will not question the need for a spiritual Master. Man needs a Master. It's your choice to select a spiritual Master or an unenlightened person as your Guru. If you are not guided by your Master, some one will guide you and if that person is not capable, you will suffer.

If you choose a political person as your Master he will rule you by fear; if you choose some other celebrity, he might rule you by greed. Only a spiritual Master rules you with love, and liberates you.

A small story:

A doctor, an engineer and a politician were arguing about whose profession was the oldest. The doctor said his was the oldest, because God created Eve from Adam's rib. The engineer disagreed and said that his was the oldest, because he first had to create Adam from chaos.

'Ah!', said the politician, who do you think created the chaos?!!
You will be ruled by those who create chaos! They infuse fear, greed and fantasies in you. They present these as fulfillment of your desires: the way you want to live, on stage, on screen.

A spiritual Master liberates you from greed, fear and fantasies.

You are all courageous, intelligent and fortunate to follow a spiritual Master. When you follow others as your masters, they do not present themselves as your teachers, yet cunningly control and direct you; whereas a spiritual Master liberates you from bondage.

He who leads from darkness to light is the Master, the Guru.

The ancient Hindu scriptures called Upanishad are the essence of the Veda, knowledge that was directly experienced by enlightened sages. Upanishad literally means to sit with the Master. You expand in universal consciousness by sitting with the Master. When you fall in love with the Master, you rise in consciousness.

The relationship with the Master transcends time and space; it is eternal. The Master-disciple relationship cannot be destroyed by the advent of science and knowledge, because it is the means to Truth, and anything that leads to the Truth is eternal and cannot die. Masters deliver the Truth to humanity.

When your Mother teaches you to say 'ma' or 'amma' (mother) she becomes your first Master. It's only after that point that you realize she is your Mother. That's why the status of the Master is placed before Mother, Father and God, and he is your first relationship. His is also the last relationship; upon enlightenment, the Master and disciple merge into a common energy.

Nothing I taught you so far in my various programs of meditation is as solid as this subject. What I have really wanted to say has always been on this Master-disciple relationship. However, unless you have done some of my courses, you would not have understood this. Now at least some of you are willing to listen. And so many more will come in future.

If you qualify, you can listen, enjoy, and transform. If not, you may relax and disappear. You are taking the jump. If you connect, relax and celebrate.
There are three levels at which I have taught. In the elementary courses that I had earlier taught, such as the Life Bliss Program, where I taught meditation techniques to energize the energy centers or chakras, of the mind-body system, you see the Master and listen to him. In the next level, the Nithyananda Spurana Program where I describe my experiences about death and take you through the process of eliminating past memories that impede your progress in life, you relate more closely with the Master. Later at the Healing Initiation, where you seek to be a disciple and I accept you as my disciple, you identify more with me and I take responsibility for your spiritual progress. Now, here, you are being with the Master. Watch my body and language so that you may imbibe.

A disciple asked his Zen Master, 'Can you teach me swimming?' The Master said, 'No, I cannot teach you, but you can learn from me.' What he meant was, 'You will gain courage by watching me, then you can jump in and swim. I cannot teach you, you have to learn.'

Enlightenment cannot be taught, but you can learn. You gain trust by watching the Master. You develop trust. You feel, 'If he can be enlightened why can't I?' Be with the Master. Behave like the Master, with a deep intense desire to seek.

It's not imitation; it's imbibing. Imbibe Nithyananda.

To imbibe, you have to do nothing; just be here. I am such a strong personality that there is no gate that will not open for me. You will imbibe Nithyananda. Relax, relate, celebrate.

Swami Vivekananda said: Awake, Arise and stop not till the goal is reached.

I say: ***Arise, Awake, STOP, the goal is reached!***

It is over a year since we first heard our Master on the Siva Sutras and over six months since he spoke to us at length on the Master-disciple relationship. Much has changed with many of us since then. Everything around the Master seems to have changed. There are new ashrams in many parts of the world now. The Bangalore ashram's landscape has changed and will keep changing. Every new structure that comes up falls short of space requirements even as it is opened up for use. Followers have multiplied many folds. Soon two levels of programs, perhaps even three that the Master used to conduct himself barely a year ago will be conducted by ordained *Acharyas* (Teachers).

Yet, despite all his warnings about how he cannot be taken for granted and how he will never be the same, the Master has remained the same. For one thing, all that one can be certain about him is the uncertainty about him. That has not changed. Each moment with him and around him is different, unpredictable, an adventure of the mind and spirit. For another, the sheer compassion that is his hallmark has not changed.

Nithyananda's mission in life is very simple. He is the rower of the boat that ferries us across the ocean of life's illusions; destroyer of the cycle of life and death. He is the *kalabhairava* who carries our spirits across time and space tirelessly with compassion.

He has declared in many a Nithyananda Spurana Program:

What I say to you is the Truth. At any point in time that you lose consciousness, be it at death or in a medical emergency, I shall be by your side. If it is at death, I shall guide you through your passage. If you do not wish to be reborn, you shall never have to be reborn again. If you wish to be reborn, you shall be reborn as what you wish to be.

My heart melts each time I hear him. My entire being overflows with gratitude to my Master, paraphrasing the words of Ramana about Arunachala: What have I done to deserve you? What can I offer to you that could be of any value to you? I have been so lucky. I have bought your grace for a pittance; your grace that millions cannot buy, I have now bought just by surrendering myself to you. It is yours to buy too.

As the Master has said, 'I am not on sale for wealth; but you can buy me with your love.'

It is not by accident that you are reading this book. It is the beginning of a journey, where the path is important and the goal is irrelevant.

We hope that this journey has been of value, inspiring you the reader further of your own path of inner discovery.

Nithyanandam! Be in eternal Bliss!

APPENDIX

Nithyananda

Nithyananda is an enlightened master and modern mystic amidst us today. He is on a mission to re-establish the science of inner bliss on planet Earth.

Born in Arunachala, South India, Nithyananda demonstrated a strong and unswerving passion for Realization of the Self even as a child. He immersed himself in daily meditation and sought the company of enlightened masters and teachers.

Nithyananda's meditation practices led to his first deep spiritual experience at age 12, which profoundly changed his life. In his own words, "It was an experience of utter bliss, serene calmness and connectedness with the Universe. I could see in a panoramic vision encompassing all 360 degrees around me, with my eyes closed. Further, I had a vivid experience of being everywhere, in the rocks, in the trees… everywhere! Just as we feel alive inside our own skin, I felt alive in the entire Cosmos."

Nithyananda left home at age 17 and embarked on an arduous journey towards Self-realization. Wandering across the length and breadth of India and Nepal and covering thousands of miles, mostly by foot, he studied *Yoga*, *Tantra* and other Eastern metaphysical Sciences and had many profound spiritual experiences through practice of intense austerities.

After years of study and deep meditation, Nithyananda attained the state of Eternal Bliss. Today, Nithyananda is an inspiring personality for millions of people worldwide. From his own experience, he has formulated a *Technology of Bliss* to explode the Individual consciousness, to awaken man to the divinity and bliss within.

He has developed a diverse range of meditation programs devised for the modern man. Scores of people around the world have experienced radical transformation in short periods of time.

To restore balance to body, mind and spirit, and to give the tools to live a creative and productive life guided by intuition and intelligence rather than instinct, Nithyananda has created programs that allow one to fall into the natural space known as meditation. He says, 'Meditation is the master key that can bring success in the material world and deep fulfillment in your space within.'

The profound techniques and processes that comprise the meditation programs help the flowering and explosion of individual consciousness. They are offered by ordained teachers, or *acharyas*, trained personally by Nithyananda. Advanced level programs are conducted by Nithyananda himself, and are a rare and unprecedented opportunity to be in the presence of the Master; to experience the deep stillness, silence and ecstasy of our inner being.

Life Bliss Foundation

Life Bliss Foundation is Nithyananda's worldwide movement for meditation and transformation. Established in the year 2003 and now spanning over 1000 centers in 33 countries, the Life Bliss Foundation continues to transform humanity through transformation of the individual.

Nithyananda Meditation Academies (NMAs) worldwide serve as spiritual laboratories where inner growth is profound and outer growth, incidental. These academies are envisioned to be a place and space to explore and explode, through a host of activities, from meditation to science. They offer *quantum spirituality*, where material and spiritual worlds merge and create blissful living; where creative intelligence stems from deep consciousness.

In the pipeline are many projects at the various academies worldwide, as well as establishment of new academies, to provide services in varied fields to humanity at large.

A diverse range of meditation programs and social services are offered worldwide through the Foundation. Free energy healing through the *Nithya Spiritual Healing system*, free education to youth, encouragement to art and culture, *satsangs* (spiritual gatherings), personality development programs, corporate programs, free medical camps and eye surgeries, free meals at all ashrams worldwide, a one-year residential spiritual training program in India, an in-house *gurukul* system of learning for children and many more such services are offered around the world.

Ananda Sevaks of the **Nithya Dheera Seva Sena (NDSS)** – volunteer force - comprising growing numbers of dedicated volunteers around the world support the mission with great enthusiasm.

Offerings from Life Bliss Foundation

Specialized meditation programs are designed and offered continuously worldwide to benefit millions of people at the levels of body, mind and spirit. Some of the meditation programs currently offered are:

Ananda Spurana Program (ASP)/Life Bliss Program (LBP)

- Energize yourself!

The initial level meditation program offered by the Foundation is the **Life Bliss Program (LBP)**, also known as the **Ananda Spurana Program (ASP)**. This is a meditation program that introduces participants to the 7 vital energy centers in our body called the *chakras*, whose functioning has a direct bearing upon our physical and mental well-being. The LBP explains the direct relationship between our emotions and these energy centers. This program facilitates effective handling of emotions, better mental clarity and a positive attitude, better interpersonal relationships, a renewed and inspired attitude towards work and above all, a blissful life.

Quantum memory program (QMP)

- Enhance your creativity

The Quantum memory program is an offering specifically for students to nurture their innate intelligence as demonstrated by a marked increase in their Intelligence Quotient (IQ), Emotional Quotient (EQ) and Spiritual Quotient (SQ).

The program exposes students to methods of enhancing their memory, visualization ability and academic performance through unique meditations, balanced diet, physical exercise, yoga, laughter and other techniques that enable the flowering of their unique intelligence and creative potential.

Nithyananda spurana program (NSP)
- Death demystified!

This program clearly elucidates the metaphysical dimensions of death. It draws the relationship between emotions of desire, fear, guilt, pain and pleasure and the seven energy bodies in human beings. It explains how each of these emotions arises from one of these seven bodies and how they work upon the departing soul as it crosses each of the seven bodies. It brings to surface all conscious and unconscious emotions that have been accumulated over the past lives, so we may be free from their clutches. The NSP creates the space for a complete spiritual rebirth that equips one with the techniques to live joyously with astounding awareness instead of deep ignorance.

Therapy programs

Our bodies are designed to be in a state of ecstatic lightness that radiates good health. Man has forgotten the art of staying healthy. Through meditation and specialized therapies, we can tune the body, mind and being to express health.

Nithyananda's meditation programs are designed to give the experiential clarity and intelligence, while therapy programs are designed to restore health and well-being. They produce immediate and long lasting results. Ranging from weight reduction therapy to de-addiction therapy and Varma Ayurvedic therapy, to homeopathy and mantra therapy, to silence therapy and aroma therapy, to flower remedies, specific programs can be tailored to suit individual requirements.

These therapies not only give relief from diseases, but are a holistic system of healing for a healthy body-mind-spirit system.

Health and Wellness Program (Arogya Spurana Program)
- Be healthy!

Good health is not just an absence of disease; it is a positive state of well-being. The Health and Wellness Program (Arogya Spurana Program) is an intense meditation program based on the integrated science of body, mind and spirit. It is an opportunity to understand that our body is not just a bio-mechanism but that which has its roots in deep consciousness and intelligence.

It takes participants through meditations that activate consciousness and create clarity about the mind-body connection, and lead to deep physical and mental healing.

Bhakti Spurana Program (BSP)
- Enrich your emotional Being

Bhakti or devotion is the language of the being. It is supreme love towards Existence or God. It frees us from base emotions, and brings equanimity of the mind and deep fulfillment. It fulfills all our wants and takes us beyond them. The Bhakti Spurana Program unfolds the path of *bhakti* to the modern man. It steers us from intellect to the being, from mundane worship to sheer intimacy - with the Divine.

Healing initiation (for Nithya spiritual healing)
- Become a healer!

Healing is restoring physical and mental health. The seven energy centers in our body called *chakras* have a deep relationship with our physical, mental and emotional well-being. ***Nithya spiritual healing*** is a method of *chakra*-based healing prayer through meditation. Nithya spiritual healers are those initiated into this science of healing, who offer this free healing service to humanity at large.

Nithyanandam

- Enlightenment-intensive

This is an intense meditation program - a unique offering of the technology of Bliss or *Nithyanandam*. All keys to the 'Experience of Enlightenment' are handed over in totality by the master himself. This is an opportunity to go beyond body and mind and experience pure consciousness.

Atma Spurana Program (ATSP)

- Connect with your Self

Man is an integral part of Existence. When he realizes this experientially, he is enlightened. This meditation program describes the five body sheaths called *koshas* that stand in the way of man realizing this truth. It offers techniques that pull our awareness through these sheaths to reach the bliss of the Self.

Dhyana Spurana Program (DSP)

- Mind is a myth; realize and liberate!

The mind is nothing but a collection of thoughts. By nature, all thoughts are unconnected, independent and illogical. The moment we realize that our thoughts are unconnected and independent, we drop our mind and become un-clutched. The moment we drop our mind, we are liberated.
This program helps to drop the mind and to remain centered in pure consciousness.

Life Bliss Technology

- Expand and Explode

Nithyananda says, 'A handful of spiritually evolved and well-centered youth is enough to transform humanity. Creating such dynamic youth is the reason for this program.'

Life Bliss Technology is a one-year residential life science program for youth aged between 18 and 30 years of age. With its roots in the Eastern system of Vedic education, this program is designed to empower the modern youth with good physical, mental and emotional health. By nurturing creative intelligence and spontaneity, and imparting vocational skills, it creates economically and spiritually self-sufficient youth.

The program aims at holistic development of the individual, and offers life science skills like leadership, technical skills like engineering and temple arts, and traditional skills like alternative therapies including Ayurveda, music therapy, life skills and applied sciences.

Above all, this is a lifetime opportunity to live and learn under the tutelage of an enlightened Master.

Nithyananda Gurukul

Nithyananda Gurukul is the loving space for children to learn and grow, and become wonderful energies of love and compassion. It creates a space for self-transformation where education is transmission of wisdom, not just knowledge. It protects and develops the innate intelligence of the child. It creates a fearless approach to life and learning. Life at the *Gurukul* is as challenging as is joyful. The children here grow to be responsible individuals, well learned and capable of facing the toughest challenges of life, while always remaining centered deeply within.

Little Anandas

Nithyananda says, 'Every child is like a flower waiting to bloom and radiate its unique beauty and fragrance. Facilitating this is the sole work of education.'

Little Anandas is a program designed for children. It offers exposure to a wide range of activities like music, dance, art, meditation and more, to open out the creativity, spontaneity and sensitivity in children. The children are facilitated to be well centered, while participating wholly in any activity outside.

Ananda Samaj

Ananda Samaj is an international community formed by the Foundation, rooted in the common ideology of experiencing and spreading inner bliss.

An ideological joint family, self-reliant economically and socially, with sound spiritual strength, Ananda Samaj is a place and space to live in the moment, without fear of the future, with service to self and humanity at a radical and profound level.

Nithyananda University

- An institution for higher learning

Nithyananda University is an upcoming university designed to be a centralized repository of the precious wisdom from the East packaged in a methodical and scientific way. Continuing the research of ancient mystics to complement scientific studies, Nithyananda University will offer education in philosophies, therapeutics, vedic studies, meditation science and more, through Bachelor of Science and Post Graduate Diploma degrees.

Nithya Yoga

Nithya Yoga is a re-presentation of Patanjali's Yoga system. It is the most ancient yet most modern system of Yoga. Its purpose is to help people un-clutch and experience eternal bliss. It is the simple and straightforward path to enlightenment. It is a technique where physical and mental healths are mere by products. Nithya Yoga is not the path *to* ecstasy but the path *of* ecstasy.

Life Bliss Galleria (Divine Shop)

The Life Bliss Galleria offers a wide range of books in English, Tamil, Kannada, Gujarati, Telugu, Hindi, Portuguese, French, Chinese and other languages, compiled from Nithyananda's discourses worldwide. Also available are discourses in cassettes, Audio CDs and Video CDs., and a host of items like photographs, shawls, chanting boxes, *malas*, chain dollars, T-shirts and so on.

Life Bliss Tree

Life Bliss Tree is a concept store that offers a range of services aimed at enriching the inner and outer worlds. Offering yoga, meditation, *satsangs* and temple worship services, for spiritual well-being, in addition the Life Bliss Tree retail stores also offer a range of eclectic products that help in the holistic growth of an individual.

A Few Limestones

- Over 2 million people touched through meditation camps world over
- Over 1 million people offered free health services in rural areas for better living
- Over 10 lakh youth touched and transformed through the Life Bliss Technology diploma program, meditation, discourses, Gurukul system of learning (ancient system of learning at the feet of the Master adapted to modern times), donation of books, volunteer-ship and one-year free residential programs
- Meditation programs in prisons and juvenile camps to reform extremist attitudes.
- Specially designed meditation programs for the global corporate world including Microsoft, AT&T, Qualcomm, JP Morgan, PetroGas, Pepsi cola, Oracle, American Association of Physicians of Indian origin (AAPI), American Telugu Association (ATA)
- 20,000 people touched everyday through free Nithya Spiritual Healing Service worldwide
- Over 10, 000 meals a day served free of charge
- Free general health camps, eye camps, eye surgeries, artificial limb donation camps etc conducted regularly.
- An international publication wing with over 200 books in 12 languages, CDs and DVDs
- Over 250 English discourses delivered by Nithyananda thus far

- Over 150 ordained *sanyasis* and *brahmacharis* of the Nithyananda order
- More than 350 teachers trained continuously by the Master himself to carry forth his message of meditation and bliss
- More than 5000 healers initiated into the Nithya Spiritual Healing system of energy healing
- More than 2000 homes, visited and energized by the master himself
- Thousands of blissful volunteers offer service for self transformation and benefit to society
- Over 1000 centers in 33 countries and 78 upcoming ashrams around the world.
- Over 30 Nithyananda Meditation Academies (NMA) worldwide
- Status of Non-profit organization acquired from the Government of the United States of America, recognized under the 501 (C) (3) category of the internal revenue services

Suggested for further reading

Guaranteed solutions

This book provides a clear understanding of our base emotions like sex, fear, worry, attention-need, jealousy, ego and discontentment. It offers understanding that can transform these base energies to higher spiritual energy so we may discover the higher dimensions of our Being. It is a revelation that can steer our life towards totality and fulfillment at the physical, mental and spiritual levels.

Bliss is the path and the goal

This book is a compilation of Nithyananda's discourses covering a range of subjects, from *How the Mind Works* to *How we abuse our bodies*, from the topic of *Surrender* to that of *Coping with the duality of material and spiritual life*. It answers many questions giving an updated understanding, kindling our inner intelligence, and tuning us to inner awareness. It is a handbook to guide us through the workings of the mind, body and being so that we may live our life in bliss.

Love is your very life **(Bhagavad Gita - chapter 12)**

Love is your very life is a chapter from the sacred scripture – The Bhagavad Gita.

"…Let us analyze our minds. If someone came up to you and told you that he loved you, you wouldn't believe it. The first thing you would try to do is figure out what he wants from you. You don't even believe you are worthy of being loved. Next, you don't believe that somebody can honestly love you, because you don't love anybody honestly. Because you are always calculative, you expect the other person also to be calculative. All our love is just skin deep; you know how deep the skin is…!"

Also released are Bhagavad Gita chapters 1, 2, 3, 4, 6, 10 and 15 have. The remaining chapters will be released soon.

Meditation is for you

In this book, Nithyananda talks on the science and art of meditation. He says, 'You don't have to learn meditation. You are already a meditator! Just remember any moment in your life when you have experienced extreme beauty. The sun rising suddenly from behind a mountain. Or the first time you hear an inexpressibly lovely piece of music. At such a moment, suddenly, you become still, wordless, totally aware. Haven't we all experienced such moments? That moment is meditation...'

The Only way out is IN

This book is a compilation of answers from Nithyananda to questions from seekers. Through penetrating answers, he gives instant clarity and restfulness to the questioning mind.

For all further details and to purchase any of the above items, please visit www.lifebliss.org or www.dhyanapeetam.org.

Our main Nithyananda Meditation Academies (NMA's)

USA:

Nithyananda Dhyanapeetam
928 Huntington Dr,
Duarte,
Los Angeles
CA 91010
USA
Ph.: 1-626 –205-3286
Email: Laashram@lifebliss.org
URL: www.lifebliss.org

Nithyananda Dhyanapeetam
820 Pollock Rd.,
Delaware,
OH 43015
Ph.: 614-571-8425 / 304-685-2240 / 740-917-4570
Email: OH@lifebliss.org

INDIA:

Nithyananda Dhyanapeetam
Nithyanandapuri
Kallugopahalli
Mysore Road, Bidadi
Bangalore - 562 109
Karnataka
INDIA
Ph.: 91 +80 65591844 / 27202084
Fax: 91 +80 27202084
Email: mail@dhyanapeetam.org
URL: www.dhyanapeetam.org

Nithyananda Dhyanapeetam
Sri Ananda Rajarajeshwari Temple,
Nithyananda Giri
Pashambanda Sathamrai Village
Shamshabad Mandal
Rangareddy District - 501 218
Andhra Pradesh
INDIA
Ph.: +8413 260311
E-mail: ap@nithyananda.org

Nithyananda Dhyanapeetam
Nithyanandapuri
Zamin Pallavaram
Chennai – 600 043
Tamil Nadu
INDIA
Ph.: 98404 27966 / 94440 19791

(Directions: Behind Tirusoolam Hill.)

Nithyananda Dhyanapeetam
Nithyanandapuri
Othaivaadai Street
Pavazhakundru
Tiruvannamalai – 606 601
Tamil Nadu
INDIA
Ph.: 94432 33789 / 94433 26202

(Directions: On Big Street (Peria theru), take the lane opposite Indian Overseas bank. This is Othaivaadai Street.)

Nithyananda Dhyanapeetam
Nithyanandapuri
2/200, Tirumangkuruchi Post
Namakkal – 637 003
Tamil Nadu
INDIA
Ph.: 94433 88437 / 93447 17629

(Directions: Near the Collector's office)

Nithyananda Dhyanapeetam
Nithyanandapuri
102, Azhagapurampudur
Salem – 636 016
Tamil Nadu
INDIA
Ph.: + 427 2449711

(Directions: Behind Sharada College)

Arunachala the hill that beckons...

While Arunachala is beyond the scope of human comprehension and calculation, how then can one know It? Surrender and He will make Himself comprehensible to you. That is the only way!

Charged with the Existential energy, Arunachala is the spiritual focal point of the entire universe. Seen here is the Arunachala hillock, which draws seekers from all over the world breaking divisions of religion, cult, creed or any dogma.

The sacred town of Tiruvannamalai (birthplace of Nithyananda) lies prostrate at the feet of the mighty Arunachala. The dwelling place of great Masters and mystics - known and unknown, this town is the most sacred pilgrimage spot ever.

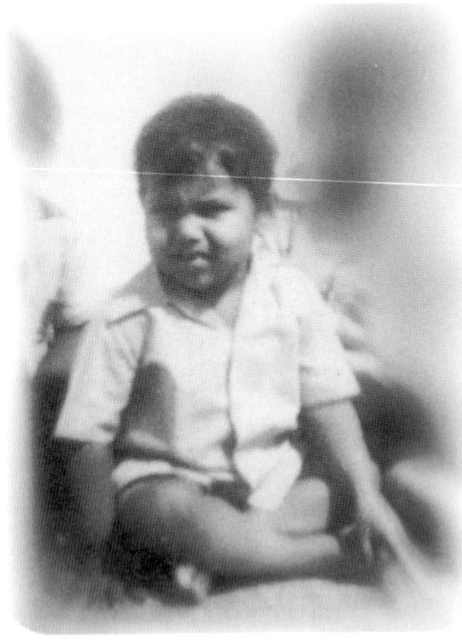

Nithyananda
as a baby - a charmer from day one!

With his two brothers. In the backdrop can be seen two of the nine temple towers of the temple of Arunachala. Wandering in the vicinity of the temple was the most enjoyable thing for him

Mother Lokanayaki and Father Arunachalam

The earliest picture of Nithyananda taken while in meditation, at the age of 10

The same picture as above touched up for archival

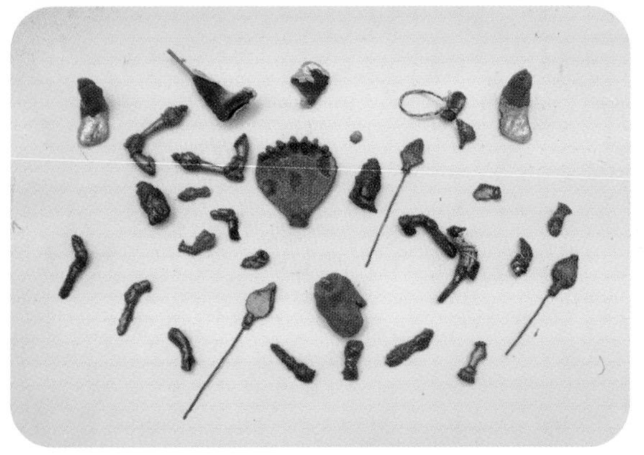

Parts of forms of deities. With these, Nithyananda would build idols with different body structures using wet earth as base material, and decorate them to his heart's content

Some of the *puja* items and clothes of deities that he used for worship

A box with the *rudraksh mala* (holy bead necklace worn by wandering mendicants) that he wore while taking the yearly pilgrimage to Sabarimala (a hill top temple dedicated to Lord Ayyappa)
His pre-monastic name 'Rajasekaran' can be seen inscribed on the box top

Nithyananda ardently worshiped deities, as live symbols of Existence. These above 5 deities, he carried with him everywhere he went and worshipped them

The Ganesa deity that ate the food served by nithyananda after devoted persistence from him

(To the left) On a family pilgrimage to Kanniyakumari, tip of India. Seen silhouetted against the sunset sky is the popular Vivekananda Rock

A group photo with one of his favorite deities - Lord Ganesa which he decorated with sandalwood paste

Raghupati Yogi, a friend, philosopher and guide to nithyananda in his spiritual quest

The deity *Parasakti* (fema personification of the Existenti energy), which appeared to hi as a vision, which he carve out of soapstor

The Kritika Mandap inside the Arunachala temple, Tiruvannamalai, where Raghupati trained him in rigorous exercises. He would make him climb the pillars several times, sometimes with the support of just one hand!

The conch teleported for him by Raghupati Yogi to demonstrate the concept of materialization

A *rudraksh* string materialized and given by Raghupati Yogi to Nithyananda, which he wore everyday. The smears of sandal paste and *kumkum* which got on to the string from his chest, can still be seen on it.

At a transcendental meditation (TM) workshop. With blazing eyes, and intense fervor, young nithyananda listens to the lecture

t a festival graced y the Master - Yogi Ram Surat Kumar, in Tiruvannamalai

The picture that he drew of himself in a fit when asked what he would be like when he grew up. One can perceive the significance of this self portrait even in this childish and hasty representation!

While Nithyananda wrote out his record notebooks at the chemistry and physics laboratories, with more zest he wrote out *mantras* and the methods of performing *puja* (offerings) and *homa* (fire rituals) with them. All this he did at an age when submitting just schoolwork was enough of a task to perform. Seen here are records that stand testimony to his peaking fervor. These *mantra* books are cyclostyled and distributed to his disciples today to aid them in performing *pujas*

With Mataji Kuppammal, spiritual guide and caretaker during his days of wandering in Tiruvannamalai

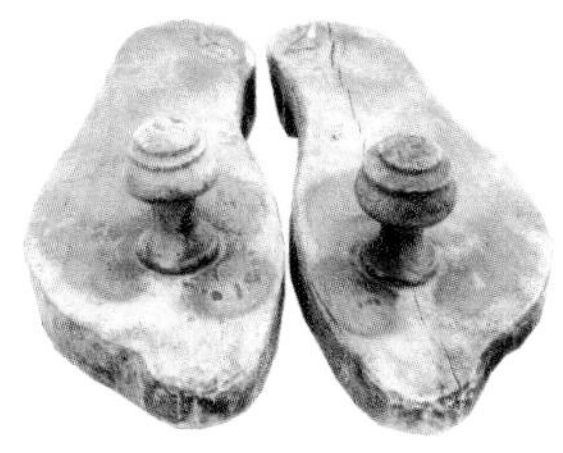

Paduka (wooden sandals normally worn by holy mendicants) given to him by Kuppammal, which he took a fancy to at a young age. Today he laughingly recalls how he would cause deafening clatter at home wearing these in the few hours he was there!

The sacred *Sri Chakra* carved by him on a copper foil having had a vision of it. When asked how he managed to carve the complex diagram so easily he explained, 'It is just nine triangles placed at different angles to each other. Once you understand the concept it becomes easy!'

Letter of initiation (in Tamil) given by Mataji Kuppammal

24.5.94

Brahma Yogini Vibuthai, who attained a high spiritual state by the grace of Maha Loo Loo Sri Sri Srila Sri Panchamukha Yogi Brahma Rishi Isakki Mahamunivar, is hereby initiating Rajasekaran, son of my loving Lokanayaki and Arunachalam, with a title, on this 10th day of the bhava year in the month of Vaikasi on Tuesday, Visakam star on Poornima (full moon) day, in response to his great enthusiasm, so he may experience the bliss that I have experienced.

Dheeksha title: Brahmasukhi

Yours,

Isakki Munivar's disciple, Viputhai alias Kuppammal Brahma Yogini

Thiruvannamalai
24.5.94

Isakki Swamigal, Guru of Mataji Kuppammal, who fostered the spiritual fever in Nithyananda

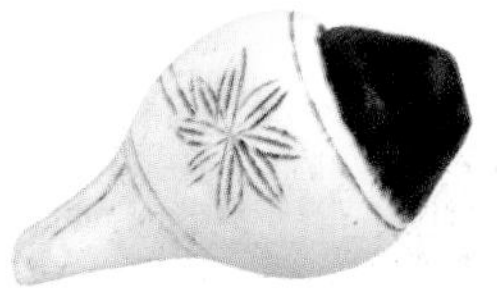

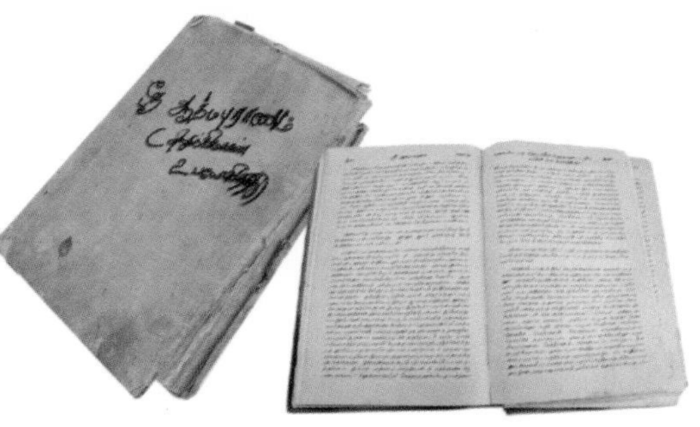

Atma Purana (a collection of Upanishad) gifted to Nithyananda by Isakki Swamigal; the first book on *Vedanta* that Nithyananda read

A conch, gifted by Isakki Swamigal, which Nithyananda used to blow while following the deity of Arunachaleshwara in procession, in the streets of Tiruvannamalai

Olai chuvadi (a manuscript made of palm leaves) containing the *rudram, chamakam* and other vedic chants, given by Isakki Swamigal to Nithyananda

Arunachala was nithyananda' everything. There was not a single crevice or rock that had not felt the fervor of his yearning. In these pictures, one can see him basking in the glory of his beloved Arunachala

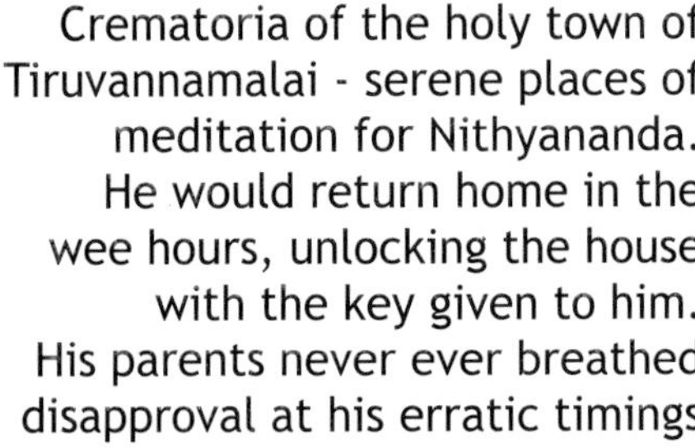

Crematoria of the holy town of Tiruvannamalai - serene places of meditation for Nithyananda. He would return home in the wee hours, unlocking the house with the key given to him. His parents never ever breathed disapproval at his erratic timings

Annamalai Swamigal disciple of Bhagwan Ramana Maharishi, who delivered the significant concept of 'beyond the body and mind' to Nithyananda in his quest for Truth.

A picture of Ramakrishna Paramahamsa another revered Master of Nithyananda - which he kept with him always

Nithyananda with his batch while at the Gudiyatham college where he did his diploma in Mechanical Engineering

The dark corner in a *mandap* (enclosure with four pillars) at the rear of the main building housing the shrine of the deity Arunachaleshwara in the temple of Tiruvannamalai, *Jiva Samadhi* (place of final resting) of Arunagiri Yogiswara, out of which Yogiswara would emerge on Nithyananda's call everyday, which prompted young Nithyananda to think there was an opening there that probably was a cave

The saffron cloth that Arunagiri Yogiswara gave Nithyananda inside the metaphysical banyan tree, which is part of the archives in the ashram at Bangalore today

Picture taken from the book 'Arunachala from Rigveda to Ramana' by A.R.Natarajan - I Edition, Dec 2002.

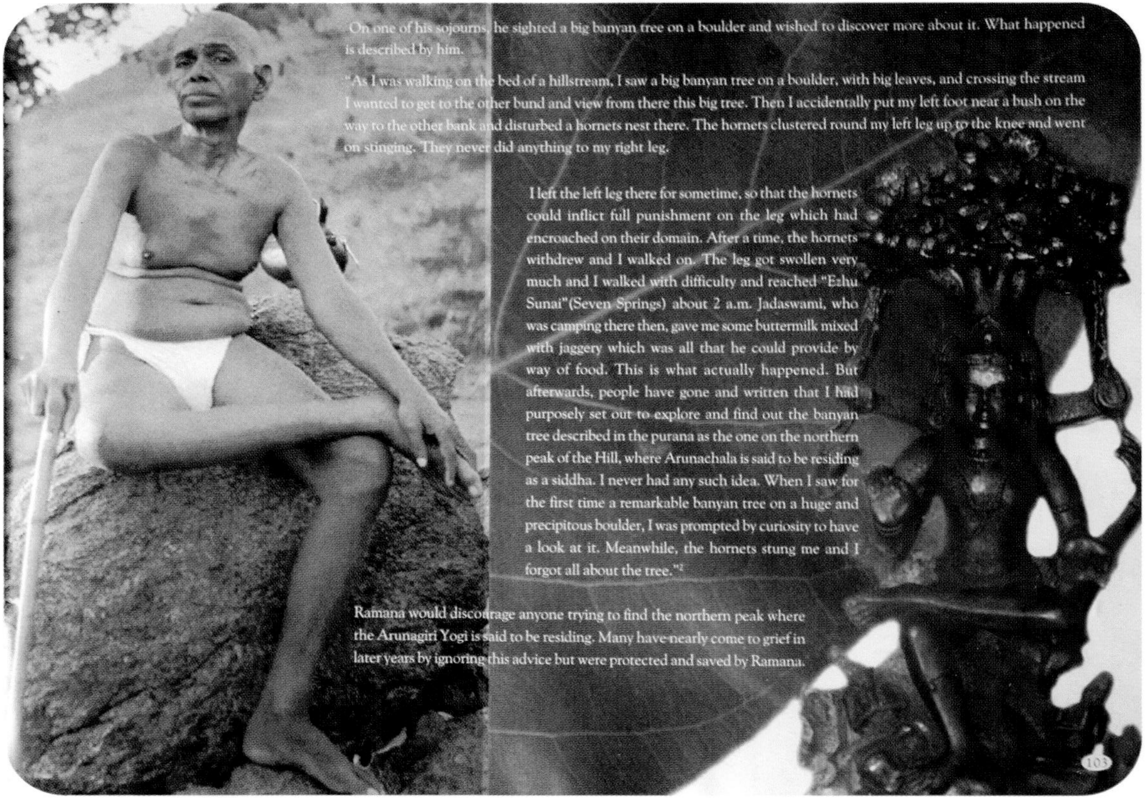

On one of his sojourns, he sighted a big banyan tree on a boulder and wished to discover more about it. What happened is described by him.

"As I was walking on the bed of a hillstream, I saw a big banyan tree on a boulder, with big leaves, and crossing the stream I wanted to get to the other bund and view from there this big tree. Then I accidentally put my left foot near a bush on the way to the other bank and disturbed a hornets nest there. The hornets clustered round my left leg up to the knee and went on stinging. They never did anything to my right leg.

I left the left leg there for sometime, so that the hornets could inflict full punishment on the leg which had encroached on their domain. After a time, the hornets withdrew and I walked on. The leg got swollen very much and I walked with difficulty and reached "Ezhu Sunai"(Seven Springs) about 2 a.m. Jadaswami, who was camping there then, gave me some buttermilk mixed with jaggery which was all that he could provide by way of food. This is what actually happened. But afterwards, people have gone and written that I had purposely set out to explore and find out the banyan tree described in the purana as the one on the northern peak of the Hill, where Arunachala is said to be residing as a siddha. I never had any such idea. When I saw for the first time a remarkable banyan tree on a huge and precipitous boulder, I was prompted by curiosity to have a look at it. Meanwhile, the hornets stung me and I forgot all about the tree."[2]

Ramana would discourage anyone trying to find the northern peak where the Arunagiri Yogi is said to be residing. Many have nearly come to grief in later years by ignoring this advice but were protected and saved by Ramana.

This is the banyan tree that Ramana Maharishi talks about that he visited onc in the Arunachala hill. He says that one day as he was walking on Arunachal hill, he was transported to a banyan tree and saw a young Yogi teaching fa older disciples under it. By implication, Ramana compared this tree and th Yogi he saw, to Lord Dakshinamurthy, incarnation of Siva Himself.

This is the same banyan tree that Sankara sang about in his Dakshinamurth Stotram; under which the South-facing young boy taught older sages i silence.

Nithyananda says:

'When I see all these references to this banyan tree under which this youn Master taught older disciples, as Arunagiri Yogiswara or Dakshinamurthy, I ar convinced that they refer to Shambhala, abode of the Sapta Rishis (seve sages), the cosmic energy center.

One can reach Shambhala from Tapovan, which is over 17,500 feet in th Himalayas beyond Gangotri and Gomukh. With the Master's help one can reac Shambhala from anywhere. The enlightened master can act as an airstrip t take you to that space at any time. The airstrips from where you can fly t Shambhala are called energy fields. The banyan tree at Bidadi (Nithyananda ashram outside Bangalore) is one such energy field to take off.

However, Shambhala is not on this earthly plane. Shambhala is an experienc that is spiritual. That is what Ramana saw and I saw with Arunagiri Yogiswara The tree that we both saw is the same banyan tree at Bidadi in our ashram.

The banyan tree that Ramana Maharishi refers to, and the banyan tree a Bidadi, are like airports or helipads to take off and reach the spiritual plan where Arunagiri Yogiswara resides in pure consciousness, as Dakshinamurth 'Siva' Himself.'